Do Not Be Afraid

Bishops and Young Clergy
Share Signs of Resurrection
and Words of Hope

Edited by
John E. Harnish

Cass Community Publishing House
an imprint of
David Crumm Media, LLC
Canton, Michigan

For more information and further discussion, visit
www.ccpublishinghouse.org

Copyright © 2015 by Cass Community Publishing House
All Rights Reserved
ISBN: 978-1-939880-96-3

Cover art and design by
Rick Nease
www.RickNeaseArt.com

Published By
Cass Community Publishing House
an imprint of
David Crumm Media, LLC
42015 Ford Rd., Suite 234
Canton, Michigan, USA

For information about customized editions, bulk purchases or
permissions, contact Cass Community Publishing House at
ccumcac@aol.com.

Contents

Dedication

This book is dedicated to the young men and women of the 21st century who have committed their lives to the work of Christ and the ordained ministry of The United Methodist Church. To them we offer the commission John Wesley gave to George Shadford in 1773 as he set sail for the colonies:

The time has arrived for you to embark. I let you loose, George, on the great continent of America. Publish your message in the open face of the sun and do all the good you can.

Letters of John Wesley, **vol. 13**

— John E. Harnish

Praise For
Do Not Be Afraid

The United Methodist Church has a wonderful heritage as a Christian movement. This book tells some stories of hope as the UMC tries to map its way forward. May the Holy Spirit continue to blow through the UMC and give us strength to face the challenges honestly and embrace the possibilities faithfully.

Dr. Jack Jackson, E. Stanley Jones Associate Professor of Evangelism, Mission and Global Methodism, Claremont School of Theology, California.

~

A fresh Wind of the Spirit is blowing on the earth and in the Church today! It is a Wind giving us eyes to see, ears to hear, and courage to act. It is rekindling the flame of renewal, offering us a future and a hope, and re-centering us in our mission. This book provides multiple vantage points to see this and to rejoice. The combination of bishops and younger clergy is a powerhouse of insight and encouragement. Read this book as if your life and ministry depend upon it. They do!

Dr. Steve Harper, retired Dean of the Orlando Campus of Asbury Theological Seminary and prolific author.

~

Do Not Be Afraid is a welcome contribution to a church that longs to hear the good news of a "future with hope." Thoughtful essays by both experienced church leaders and fresh young voices point to exciting new ways in which God's reign in Jesus Christ is being fulfilled in our time. Amid the death and decline of many of the "old ways," the authors describe creative new ministries in the community, renewed congregations and ordinary people whose lives have been transformed by Jesus Christ. *Do Not Be Afraid* is a book to lift your spirits, revive your imagination and approach the future with joy.

Bishop Janice Riggle Huie, Dallas, Texas.

~

I am excited about the future. God is bringing resurrection in formally dying places. Now in the fourth decade of ministry at Ginghamsburg Church, I am more passionate than ever about the call to local church ministry, young folk who are heeding God's call and the stories of resurrection shared in this book.

Michael Slaughter, Lead Pastor, Ginghamsburg Church, Tipp City, Ohio.

~

As humanity in the church world tries to recreate itself in surprising and amazing ways, the writers of this book describe endings and beginnings that offer hope for the future. Christ embodied the process of moving from life through death to resurrection. There is great hope in the revelatory expressions of Christ's resurrection happening every day, all over the church and the world. Thanks to these writers for identifying some places and ways we can celebrate these expressions! "For surely I know the plans I have for you, says the Lord, plans for your welfare and not harm, to give you a future with hope." (Jeremiah 29:11)

Bishop Linda Lee, bishop-in-residence at Garrett-Evangelical Theological Seminary.

~

All will be heartened as they read through these pages and discover a treasure of encouraging reminders to not be afraid for the future for the United Methodist Church and its related institutions. It confronts us with the reality of needed flexibility, adaptation, major innovation, and the need to make some things brand new. However, the core beliefs of our Christian, and Wesleyan heritage remains the same. My hope and prayer for the future of our UMC is that like the many who have written on these pages, we too might respond as Mary did with the angel Gabriel, in essence saying, "I'm not sure what this means, but here I am ready to be of service in the ongoing work of God!"

Dr. Myron F. McCoy, Senior Pastor of the First United Methodist Church at the Chicago Temple and former president of St. Paul School of Theology, Kansas City.

~

It's true. A drop of 89,000 in membership is not good news. But these reflections look beyond the church as an institution in North America to the Church as the Body of Christ and the People of God sharing the good news to all of God's creation—a sign and symbol of hope in a confused and violent world. Leaders from every level of responsibility and voices from lands far and near reflect on being the Church in the 21st century. I started reading these essays thinking "Just another collection of people wringing their hands over institutional decline." I was wrong! The authors face the institution's reality honestly, but they look beyond to a clear-headed perspective on being the Church of Jesus Christ. I am glad that I kept reading. I was instructed. I was inspired.

Dr. W. Stephen Gunter, Associate and Research Professor of Evangelism and Wesleyan Studies, Duke Divinity School.

~

Do Not Be Afraid is filled with fruitful and God-led ways and examples of how God continues to do a new thing across the United Methodist Church. Using metaphors ranging from roadkill to doomsday to reference what folks are saying about the denomination, the writers continue to remind the reader that the future of the church is one filled with hope. The stories and testimonies from both young clergy and bishops show the reader how individuals have not given up hope in God, who continues to do new things around the world. While many in the denomination are paralyzed by fear and are resistant to change, these powerful and heart-warming stories demonstrate that we can always count on something new from God. Indeed, this book is a must-read for all who yearn to learn how God calls us to use imagination, fruitfulness, hope and faith for the future of the church.

The Rev. David Wilson, Choctaw, Conference Superintendent of the Oklahoma Indian Missionary Conference.

Listening for the Angels: An Introduction

At our first meeting as a writing team, Michigan Bishop Deborah Kiesey greeted us by saying, "I'm excited about this book. We've heard enough voices warning that the Church is dying. We've worried enough about whether the Church can survive. I'm ready to share some hope!" Sitting in Bishop Kiesey's office, with a half dozen bishops from around the world participating in our conference call, we could feel a spirit moving.

And she was right. In a time of bad news, hand wringing and even a few minority voices calling for the breakup of the United Methodist Church (UMC), we believe there is a need for a voice of hope. We believe we need to hear the words of the angel messenger once again, *"Do not be afraid."*

A look back ...

How did we descend into this fearful assumption that we are in a downward spiral? After all, from 12 followers 2,000 years ago, Christians now number more than 2 billion souls around the world and, in the U.S. alone, United Methodists count 8 million recently active members and more individual churches spread across the landscape than any other religious group. At the same time, we have seen the slow erosion of our membership here in the U.S. and with it, the malaise that often accompanies and exacerbates decline. Words of demise become a self-fulfilling prophecy so that in recent years, we have heard an almost constant drumbeat about the death of the Church. Sometimes it is used as the pretext for motivational speeches on Church growth or the impetus for new initiatives in branding, marketing, structural reorganization and evangelism—all well intended and sometimes even effective, but all driven by the message of malaise and demise. Sometimes it is simply said with the shaking of the head and an *oh well, what can you do?* Sometimes it is almost spoken with pride as in, *we are called to be faithful not successful,* as if our predicted death was evidence of our prophetic witness. For the most part, we treat it like the crazy uncle no one wants to acknowledge, except once a year when he shows up at the family reunion we Methodists call Annual Conference.

The most recent statistics for the denomination in the U.S. simply restate the obvious. The General Board of Global Ministries reports: "While the most recent General Minutes data follows the same general rending that has been seen for some time, the good news is that things seem to follow last year's mild moderation" (that means, I guess that we are dying slower!) "... and, even a surprising uptick in a critical indicator. The membership decline of 88,729 (-1.2 percent) was very comparable to last year, which had been a mild improvement over the previous years."

It's hard to interpret the loss of 88,729 members as good news, but it is better than some of the previous years. Still, 88,729 represents a lot of people! And it is still a loss. (See: *Background Data for Mission*, April 2014, Research Office of the General Board of Global Ministries, John Southwick, researcher.)

In 1968, the marriage of the Evangelical United Brethren and the Methodists created the United Methodist Church. In most of our Annual Conferences in America, membership has been gradually declining ever since. In the early years following the merger, we put it down to the necessary sifting and shifting that naturally takes place in such a time. We said we were just "cleaning the books," getting rid of dead wood, accounting for all those folks who flooded the Church during the salad days of the '50s but had long since left anyway. In the late '60s and early '70s we assumed the Church's prophetic witness regarding civil rights or the war in Vietnam would, of course, result in some dissatisfaction and drifting away.

Then in the '80s, when the hard truth could no longer be conveniently ignored, it became the focus of constant study, furious action and reaction. It was often the motivation for structural changes in the hope that reorganization would bring revival. In 1986, Bishop Richard Wilke wrote his book on the future of the United Methodist Church with the probing title taken from the Wesley hymn, "And Are We Yet Alive?"

The 21st century produced a plethora of plans, proposals and publications mostly coming from megachurches. Creative conferences and practical workshops multiplied. We figured if we could just adopt what the big boys were doing, we could make our own little gardens grow. So every church had to have a praise band and a video screen. Boring hymns were replaced with fluffy "7-11" praise songs (that is, seven words repeated 11 times), choirs with drab robes were downsized to worship teams with handheld mikes and worshipers brought their Starbucks instead of their starched shirts to worship. Metrics became the measure to the point that some district superintendents required a Monday morning report of worship attendance and visitors, new members and children, any number that might be important to measuring our membership goals and growth.

Sometimes it even worked.

Much of what we have done has been wonderfully creative and responsive to the needs of the times and in varying degrees we have seen real change as the Holy Spirit has worked through our sometimes feeble and fumbling attempts to discover the "new thing" God might be doing. But all of it has been set against the backdrop of the message of death and decline.

First motivation: the need for a voice of hope

In the light of this history and our present malaise, we felt there was a need for a voice of hope, a word about those places and spaces in our common life where resurrection is taking place, sometimes unnoticed, sometimes small, sometimes even ignored—but new life just the same. Where are the signs of promise? How do we live and work with hope and where does that hope come from? Can we hear the voice of the angel messenger once again saying, *"Do not be afraid"*? This has been the first motivation for this book.

Second motivation: voices of young clergy

The second motivation came from experiences each of us has had in working with young men and women who are entering the ministry these days. We have seen their vigor and vision; their passion and commitment that springs forth even in the graveyard of growth statistics. They hear all the bad news in seminary and still they come. They are confronted with it when they walk in to their first small church appointment which hasn't seen any growth in years, yet the district superintendent tells them their work will be measured by the number of new members they receive and still they come. They are told that in the "post-post-Christian" era they will not have the eager support of society or prestige in their communities and still they come. They come with hope and vitality—even joy—at the prospect of serving Christ in this present age. We have seen their passion and we feel the need to give voice to their spirit. We want to encourage them in their calling and to point to them as one of the signs of hope for the future. Instead of another how-to manual we simply want to cheer them on and let them know the Church is still a great place to follow God's calling and that ordained ministry is still a wonderful way to spend your life. In part, we write for them and for the future they will shape and build. Perhaps along with our bishops, you will hear the angel's voice speaking through them as well.

Third motivation: biblical revelation

Our third motivation comes from the underlying theme of the biblical revelation—new creation out of void, new life in unexpected places, new hope in the face of despair, all things being made new. The opening lines of the Genesis narrative envision the creative spirit of God moving over the face of the deep. Light breaks forth in the blackness. Life is born out of nothing. The poet of the Psalms and the voices of the prophets see blossoms in the waste places and streams in the dessert. They hold out the hope of redemption from the slave pits as the Lord's song is sung even in a foreign land. Finally Jesus comes. The light shines in the darkness and the promise is that darkness will never overcome it. In the birth of the Church at Pentecost, ancient traditions take on new meaning and the final promise is that in the final days God's kingdom will come on earth even as it is in heaven. The season of Advent opens with a voice crying in the wilderness and ends with the star lighting the way to new birth. The season of Lent begins in the ashes of our human frailty and ends in the glorious dawn of the first day of the week. From beginning to end, the Bible is the story of death and resurrection. It is the story of new life and hope in the most hopeless of places. We believe this is the message the Church needs to hear and the message the Church needs to share. The same message that came to Joseph and Mary and the shepherds in the fields needs to be heard today: *"Do not be afraid."*

A word about our writers

This project began in the mind and heart of the Rev. Faith Fowler. For the past 20 years, Faith has been working to bring resurrection and hope in places of death and despair. As the pastor of Cass Community United Methodist Church and the executive director of Cass Community Social Services in Detroit, she has seen it all. She has walked the streets and confronted the demons in neighborhoods of hurt and home-lessness. She has dealt with the challenges of institutional neglect and governmental gridlock that impacts the lives of men, women and children who live in poverty. She has brought vitality to an old inner-city church and literally saved the lives of thousands of persons who had no future. She is an evangelist of new life and a witness to resurrection on a daily basis.

Faith began by talking with David Crumm, co-founder of Front Edge Publishing, editor of ReadTheSpirit online maga-zine, and the former religion editor of the Detroit Free Press. David knows the city of Detroit, the United Methodist Church, the ecumenical religious world and publishing. He was eager to help launch the project. So, Faith gathered us as a team around the vision for a book that would give voice to the hope of the Gospel by calling on a collection of bishops to speak from their experience in their various settings.

We carefully selected a group of bishops who represent the broad range of United Methodism—from the Pacific Coast to upstate New York; from the rapidly growing Church of Africa to the minority Methodists of Northern Europe; from the Sun Belt of Florida to the Rust Belt of Michigan and the Great Plains in between. With one exception, they are active bishops whose voices are not frequently heard beyond their own areas. The exception is a retired bishop who has worked closely with seminary students and newly appointed clergy at the beginning of their ministries with a passion for those on the margins of society. As bishops of the Church, we look to them for the word of hope and the message of resurrection.

Finally, we invited a group of young clergy, persons who recently graduated from seminary and are serving their first appointment, to offer their vision and their hopes for the Church. From across the nation, they speak with a passion and commitment that will inspire your hope for the future.

Introducing our publishing house

Cass Community Publishing House is another expression of the creative vision of the Rev. Fowler and Cass Social Services. As a way of funding ministry and providing jobs for persons who would be otherwise unemployed, Cass has developed a set of "green industries" which benefit the environment as well as the employees and the Cass program. Collecting discarded tires from empty lots and turning them into mud mats and sandals; recycling paper and x-rays; an exercise gym with stationary bicycles which generate electricity; and small cottage industries for the developmentally disabled are examples of the Cass enterprises. Cass Community Publishing House helps to provide a forum for voices that would otherwise go unheard and it supports Cass United Methodist Church. All proceeds will go to their ministry in the inner city of Detroit, bringing light in the darkness and hope in the place of fear.

Our desire is that this book will stimulate the conversation and help local congregations identify those places where there is hope of new life and where resurrection is taking place in the Body of Christ. We seek to encourage young clergy and lay leaders. We seek to be a witness to resurrection so that the Church might once again hear the angelic message: *"Do not be afraid."*

—*John E. Harnish*

John E. Harnish is a United Methodist pastor whose 43-year ministry has circled the globe, including seven years as the associate general secretary of the General Board of Higher Education and Ministry. While in that role, he was instrumental in the implementation of the 1996 ordering of ministry and he was involved in the planting of the two newest United Methodist seminaries in the world in Estonia and Russia. For over a decade he served on the board of trustees for the Baltic Methodist Theological Seminary and is currently a trustee at Methodist-related Adrian College. Dr. Harnish is a graduate of Asbury College and Asbury Theological Seminary and was awarded a Doctor of Divinity degree from Garrett-Evangelical Theological Seminary. He served churches ranging from a three-point charge in rural Pennsylvania to the position of senior pastor at two of Michigan's largest United Methodist churches in Ann Arbor and Birmingham. Now retired, he lives in northwest Michigan with his wife, Judy, a retired public school principal.

"Do Not Be Afraid"

Somewhere along the way I read or heard a comment attributed to Parker Palmer that went something like this: "The message of the Bible can be summarized with these words: fear not." I wish I knew for certain that Palmer had said it. If he did, he may have well been quoting someone else. Nevertheless the words ring true for me. I believe that you can read through the Scriptures of our faith and come away with a clear sense that a part of what God wants to say to us is, *"Do not be afraid."* The apostle Paul, in addressing the Church while mentoring and encouraging Timothy, reminds us that the fear that makes us cower in a corner, tuck tail and run or host a pity party, does not come from God. He boldly declares in 2 Timothy 1:7: *"For God did not give us a Spirit of fear but of power, love and self-control."*

Do Not Be Afraid is a welcome contribution to a growing body of work that invites the United Methodist Church to claim a "future with hope." This collection of essays and short witnesses from voices that are newer and fresher as well as those that are more seasoned reflect a wide landscape and truly diverse contexts of ministry practice and leadership. The clarion call to "fear not" does not ignore the reality the United Methodist Church faces in the 21st century. This book offers a lot of truth-telling and naming of current reality and then proceeds without apology or hesitation to point to the many, many ways that God is at work through the Church doing what God does: "making a way in the wilderness, and rivers in the desert" (Isaiah 43:19).

The invitation to live and work in hope is grounded in the trust and confidence that the God we serve has a track record over a long arc of time. God makes ways where there appears to be no way and God has been doing this work for far longer than there has been a Church, much less the United Methodist Church. We are called anew to affirm our faith in this God. Truth be told, we haven't got a prayer of being faithful and fruitful Christian disciples or a faithful and fruitful Church unless we have a relentless trust in God. Anything we accomplish apart from God will not last. For that matter it shouldn't last. Our hope and any hopeful future worth having must find its home and its heart in the triune God.

Like all of the contributors to *Do Not Be Afraid*, I have the responsibility, privilege and joy of being a part of a lot of configurations of church. Often I am there to preach and celebrate significant markers in the life of the community. At the close of many of those occasions I have the opportunity to pronounce the benediction or offer a blessing over the people. I have several benedictions or blessings that I use that are committed to memory. I have others still that I draw from that are printed out on cards or pieces of paper slipped into the back of my Bible. Most of the benedictions I use are either direct quotes from Scripture or are based on Scripture verses. One of my favorites is from Romans 15:13: "May the God of hope fill you with all joy and peace in believing, so that you may abound in hope by the power of the Holy Spirit." When I speak, hear or read these words my spirit leaps with an assurance that the Church's hope is in God and that God is working to fill the church to overflowing with joy, peace and hope.

With gratitude to the dreamers of this project and all the contributors to this volume I commend it to you with the prayer that God will use it to quicken hope in all of us until fear has no room in which to maneuver or thrive.

—*Gregory Vaughn Palmer*

Bishop Gregory Vaughn Palmer currently serves as the episcopal leader for the West Ohio Area of the United Methodist Church. Originally from Philadelphia, he graduated from George Washington University and Duke Divinity School. He has received honorary degrees from Baldwin-Wallace College, Iowa Wesleyan College, Simpson College, Hood Theological Seminary and Garrett-Evangelical Theological Seminary. Previously, he served as bishop in the Iowa and Illinois Areas of the UMC.

CHAPTER 1

The Gift of Spirit-Led Imagination

IMAGINE A CHURCH that knows and shares unimaginable love. Imagine a Church that claims unimaginable power. Imagine a Church that breaks down walls, meets people where they are, and boldly proclaims the power of the Gospel message. It's time to move out of our comfort zones, and dream of something more than our current reality.

Imagination is essential, and the movie *Chicken Run* helps us understand why. In *Chicken Run*, dozens of chickens are held captive in a prisoner-of-war-like camp at Tweedy Farms. A chicken named Ginger has her heart set on something better, and keeps devising plans for the chickens to escape. Ginger knows that when a hen's egg production is down they will face the chopping block, and she dreams of a place where the grass is green and the chickens can be free. In a chicken coop organizational meeting, Ginger shares her new escape plan with the chickens. They have already tried going under the fence, and now they will find a way to fly over the fence. Ginger encourages the chickens to imagine a place on the other side of the fence where there is no farmer, no egg count, and no chopping block.

Some of the chickens have a hard time seeing the place Ginger imagines. One chicken says, "Perhaps we should just try not escaping."

Ginger responds: "What kind of life do we have just laying eggs until we get wacked and stuffed. … Don't you see? The fences aren't just in the yard; they're in your mind."

The chicken gruffly answers back, "The chances of us getting out of here are a million to one."

"There's still a chance then," Ginger replies.

Webster's Dictionary defines imagination as "the act or power of forming a mental image of something not present to the senses or never before wholly perceived in reality." Ginger is able to dream of someplace better, even though she has never experienced it herself. She hopes in this future despite the doubts of her friends, and she is not afraid to share her vision with others, even though she's living in the shadow of the fence that presents her biggest obstacle. We are called to this kind of imagination.

Two foundational truths

We are the Church of Jesus Christ. Christ is our hope and vision. Our spirit-led imagination is based on two foundational truths we must stand upon. First, we have been chosen by God. We have been chosen by God's amazing grace. God loves us just as we are, no matter who we are or what we have done or not done. Through our faith in Jesus Christ, God promises to erase our transgressions and makes us *new*!

Second, we have been called by God. We have been called to claim that amazing grace; called to surrender to it and be transformed by it, *so that* we can be used by God to share that amazing grace with the world around us. God calls us—in order to use us—*so that* others may know they too have been chosen and called. That's who we are as the Church of Jesus Christ. That is our purpose, our destiny and our reality.

One of the fears I have for the Church of the 21st century is that we have lost our spiritual imagination. We don't fully believe we've been chosen and called by God, and thus we don't live the power of these truths within our lives and toward the lives of those we encounter day by day. My greatest hope for the Church is that we will truly claim these truths and experience the fullness of who God has called us to be.

Remembering Webster's definition of imagination mentioned earlier in this chapter, it's time for us to imagine. It's time for us to claim what God says is true about our identity and purpose. This is the moment for us to free ourselves from the fences in our minds and to have a spirit-inspired imagination greater than Ginger's dream for the chickens to fly to freedom. It's time for us to imagine God's reality for God's people and God's Church.

Imagining God's new reality

In a *Peanuts* comic strip, Charlie Brown, Lucy and Linus are lying on the ground, looking up into the sky. Lucy says, "If you use your imagination, you can see lots of things in the cloud formations. What do you think you see, Linus?"

Linus responds, "Well, those clouds up there look like the map of the British Honduras on the Caribbean. And that cloud looks a little like the profile of Thomas Eakins the famous painter and sculptor. And that group of clouds over there gives me the impression of the stoning of Stephen. I can see the apostle Paul standing here to one side."

Lucy congratulates him, "Uh huh, that's very good. What do you see in the clouds, Charlie Brown?"

Charlie Brown replies, "Well, I was going to say I saw a ducky and a horsey, but I changed my mind."

What kind of God-given reality will we imagine? What difference will it make?

As we seek to be the Church of Jesus Christ, we must ask: What is the reality that we know and live?—and then imagine the reality God has in mind for us. The prophet Jeremiah spoke to a people in exile, telling about the hope and future that should guide their living and become their reality in the midst of that exile. His words in chapter 29, verse 11 speak similarly to the Church of our time: *"For I know the plans I have for you, declares the Lord, plans for welfare and not for calamity to give you a future and a hope."*

Some would say there is calamity in the United Methodist Church. They would tell you our future looks bleak and that hopelessness is ruling the day. The reality is that our beloved United Methodist Church in the United States is in decline and has been for some time. Since the beginning of the United Methodist Church in 1968, we have not grown by one person in the U.S. Removal of members by death and transfer to other churches outnumber people being received in our congregations by profession of faith. We are burying more people than we are baptizing. People who once sat in our pews are missing and young adults are almost nonexistent in most of our congregations. We have too often given in to managing the decline that is our current reality.

But, God's reality is what we must begin to imagine. God has chosen us! God has called us! God will use us in the midst of exile and decline to be God's people and to be God's Church. Even in times of seeming hopelessness, God will use us to make disciples of Jesus Christ so that the world might be changed for the glory of God!

In 2010, the Upper New York Conference of The United Methodist Church was born. The honest truth is that birth was necessary because of our numerical decline—because of **our** reality. But we have a choice: We can hold on to our current reality, dig in our heels and fatefully follow the path we believe has been laid out for us—or we can imagine God's reality. We can begin to imagine a new future based on Jeremiah's words: "For I know the plans I have for you, declares the Lord, plans for welfare and not for calamity to give you a future and a hope."

God's reality is one that says:

> *Build houses and live in them and plant gardens and eat their produce. Take wives and become the fathers of sons and daughters and take wives for your sons and give your daughters to husbands ... multiply and do not decrease. Seek the welfare of the city where I have sent you into exile and pray to the Lord on its behalf.*
>
> *—Jeremiah 29:5-7*

God's reality is found in the words of Jesus to Peter after Peter's confession of who Jesus was:

> *You are Peter and upon this rock I will build my church and all the powers of hell will not conquer it. I will give you the keys of the kingdom of heaven and whatever you bind on earth shall have been bound in heaven, and whatever you loose on earth shall have been loosed in heaven.*
>
> *—Matthew 16:18-19*

What should we do?

God's reality is found in the Book of Acts on the day of Pentecost. Peter shared the reality of Jesus, and those who listened were pierced to the heart and responded: *"What should we do?"* Peter invited them to change their hearts and lives by receiving the Holy Spirit. The response on that day added about 3,000 souls to the movement of "Jesus followers."

The Upper New York Conference of the United Methodist Church is seeking to live out God's calling. Before we look to specific ministries that may be engaged or even strategies that may be employed, we must look to God's call. We must engage our imagination to explore what God has for us. God's reality, rather than our own human reality, must become the path that leads us forward. We believe deeply that God desires to work through us to offer the hope, significance, purpose and life that is found in Jesus Christ to all.

We have to first claim that reality for ourselves—live it deeply and be owned by it totally. The Upper New York Conference is still finding its identity. As portions of four previous Conferences experience the transformation into a new organism/organization, there is work we must continue to do amongst ourselves. The leaders of Upper New York have identified the three most important things we must do to strengthen our current reality as we move toward God's reality. As we continue to discover our identity as the Upper New York Annual Conference, almost all our decisions are guided by whether or not they help us to accomplish these three vital things:

1.   Claiming our spiritual identity
2.   Deepening relationships with one another
3.   Developing clarity of direction and purpose

Alongside this essential work, we also must look to the reality of our mission field. In 2013, the Barna Group published a study, entitled, "The Most Post-Christian Cities in America." In the study, they tracked 15 metrics related to faith. These metrics speak to the lack of Christian identity, belief and practice. In this study, the definition of "post-Christian" was based on the percentage of the population that meets at least 60 percent of the Barna Group's post-Christian metrics. Those metrics are as follows:

1.   Do not believe in God
2.   Identify as atheist or agnostic
3.   Disagree that faith is important in their lives
4.   Have not prayed to God (in the last year)
5.   Have never made a commitment to Jesus

6.   Disagree that the Bible is accurate
7.   Have not donated money to a church (in the last year)
8.   Have not attended a Christian church (in the last year)
9.   Agree that Jesus committed sins
10. Do not feel a responsibility to "share their faith"
11. Have not read the Bible (in the last week)
12. Have not volunteered at church (in the last week)
13. Have not attended Sunday school (in the last week)
14. Have not attended a religious small group (in the last week)
15. Do not participate in a house church (in the last year)

According to this study, 5 of the top 25 post-Christian cities are located within the bounds of the Upper New York Annual Conference. That is our reality. Some have viewed this reality as a negative, pointing to the potential ineffectiveness of congregations. Others have allowed this information to further feed a stereotype that the culture around them is "not interested" in faith or the things of God. As leaders in Upper New York, we have used this study to point to the great possibilities and potential we have to reimagine the way we "do church" and to find more effective and relevant ways to share the story of God's amazing love through Jesus Christ. Even more significant is the fact that the number one and number two post-Christian cities identified in the study are within the bounds of the Upper New York Annual Conference.

That is our reality. But we are seeking God's reality and desiring to move toward it!

Currently, leaders of the Upper New York Annual Conference are engaged in a process of mission-mapping (also known as strategic planning). We understand our core purpose to be "making disciples of Jesus Christ for the transformation of the world", and we are asking the critical questions that will cause us to live out that purpose fully. Disciples are made by congregations (not by Annual Conferences or by districts) and we want to help equip people to do this important work in their communities.

As we try to imagine God's reality, we must be clear about the primary tasks of an annual conference. For a year and a half, I led intentional conversations in each of the 12 districts of the Upper New York Area. These conversations began with a clear call to reclaim our mandate to make disciples of Jesus Christ! The conversations continued by inviting clergy and laity to focus on and look at some questions that allowed us to discover some common understanding around terms we often toss around in the life of The United Methodist Church. The questions were these:

- What is a transformational leader?
- How do we together create a culture that recruits, equips, and multiplies transformational leaders?
- What is a vital congregation?
- How do we together create a culture that resources and multiplies vital congregations?
- What is a disciple of Jesus Christ?
- How do we together more effectively live our mission of making disciples of Jesus Christ for the transformation of the world?

These conversations helped us to build a shared foundation and to define the outcomes we are aiming for, as we try to imagine how to live in God's reality. One of the first steps was for us to become very clear about the purpose and the primary tasks of an annual conference. Since arriving in Upper New York, everywhere I go, I remind others and myself that local churches make disciples. The annual conference is a partner with local churches in living out that mission, but the mission happens as individuals in local congregations build relationships with one another and those within their community.

Our Mission Map clearly identifies the mission of the local church and the purpose of the conference, by using these words:

"The mission of the Church is to make disciples of Jesus Christ for the transformation of the world. Local Churches provide the most significant arena through which disciple making occurs." (From "*The Book of Discipline of The United Methodist Church*," paragraph 120)

"The purpose of the annual conference is to make disciples of Jesus Christ for the transformation of the world by equipping its local churches for ministry and by providing a connection for ministry beyond the local church; all to the glory of God." (From "*The Book of Discipline of The United Methodist Church*," paragraph 601)

Standing upon that foundation of purpose for the local church and the annual conference, we have identified the following primary tasks of the annual conference:

- Recruit and equip transformational clergy and lay leadership so that our congregations will joyfully and faithfully live out the vision of Upper New York.
- Connect local churches with tools and practices for disciple-making in the 21st century, as well as re-forming the Church for vitality, relevance and fruitfulness.
- Nurture a planting culture where people recognize the movement of the Spirit to begin new faith communities. This includes providing the training and resources for people to plant sustainable communities of faith.
- Align resources to support the purpose of the annual conference and the mission of the local church and implement a system of accountability for mission and ministry at all levels.
- Communicate how we share a common mission as United Methodist Christians in the 21st century.

What difference will it make?

As we begin to focus on these tasks, we must ask ourselves how we will know when God's goal has been achieved. How will we be different? How will our transformation allow us to courageously be used by God for the transformation of the world? Defining what this new reality will look like is a work in progress, but my beginning hopes are that we will be a people who deeply know that we are called by God for relationship; that we will boldly claim our connection to one another in love and we will celebrate that our connection to Jesus Christ bears fruitfulness and effectiveness. As the Body of Christ is radically transformed, the ways in which we live out our mission and ministry will radically change as well. Those changes will result in indicators of vitality and growth. I pray for the day when we as the people of Upper New York Annual Conference will be able to claim movement from our current reality to God's preferred reality. Here, again, we must use our imagination to identify indicators of transformation. They include:

- Authentic, relevant worship that results in increased worship attendance
- Increasing the number of transformational clergy and lay leaders by offering new training to current leaders as well as recruiting new leaders with fresh ideas
- Increasing the number of local congregations who have the following: adult professions of faith, small groups focused on maturing discipleship and hands-on ministries of mission
- Creating effective children's, youth and young adult ministries that connect with the community and increase total number of children, youth and young adult participants

- Helping congregations identify their unique context for ministry. They will discover what God is already doing in their midst and develop a pathway to further vitality
- Increasing racial and ethnic diversity and gender equality in our faith communities
- Increasing giving for ministry and mission by fostering a culture of generosity in local congregations
- Increasing the number of congregations engaged in hands-on justice and mercy ministries, both in the community and around the world

As we imagine a new reality based on our mission, we also need to talk about resources. While we have been consistent in stating that the mission of "making disciples of Jesus Christ for the transformation of the world" happens through the ministry of local congregations, the structure of our annual conference has spoken a different message. We are now attempting to align our conference structure to emphasize partnership, equipping, resourcing and accountability. For example, we are shifting to make the districts the center of our structure. District superintendents will move from managers to missional strategists; conference staff will be deployed to local congregations, districts, and regions to equip people with resources based on their identified needs and goals.

Using the concept of team leadership that is built around the purposes of loving, learning and leading, we are moving toward district leadership teams led by the district superintendents. Teams must do the hard work of building relationships with one another and engaging in spiritual formation so that they can lead others toward the possibility and reality of God. Teams wrestle with this question: "What is God already doing in our region and what do our leaders and faith communities need to join that work?" The answers to this question will help us allocate resources and training to meet the needs of our districts.

As we imagine a new reality for the United Methodist Church in our area, we in Upper New York hope to increase vital congregations and transformational leaders. The cabinet and the Board of Ordained Ministry led us in realigning our Conference staff structure to create two full-time positions that focus on these critical areas. Our new Director of Vital Congregations and Director of New Faith Communities are already helping our congregations bear much fruit. We are daring to live into God's reality, and we are witnessing transformation.

Another exciting development is the success of "Hand to Plow." Hand to Plow is similar to "The Healthy Church Initiative" being used in other parts of our Methodist connection. Hand to Plow consists of peer-learning groups focused on clarity of purpose, spiritual formation and building leadership skills for both clergy and lay leaders. Consultants then guide local congregations in examining their current reality and imagining what God's reality might hold—as well as identifying concrete steps for how to move toward God's reality in their lives and ministry. In our first round of peer learning groups, over 700 clergy and lay leaders (representing 140 congregations) participated. Our first round of church consultations included 13 congregations.

To live into God's reality, we must transform existing congregations—but that alone will not be enough. We have a goal to create 100 new faith communities through 2020. At the time of this writing, 22 new faith communities have launched and 15 are in various stages of planning and development. This is an exciting sign of possibility and transformation.

God's reality is not found only in the Upper New York Annual Conference. You may find this new reality in your own Annual Conference, your own district and your own local congregation when you help someone grow in their faith. When you make a commitment to help people in your congregation grow in their relationship with God, that's God's reality. When you make a choice to do whatever it takes so that at least one more person—one more person like you, or one more person different from you—has a chance to know Jesus, that's God's reality! That is our mission— that is our purpose!

It's time to discover God's reality

What do we see? What reality do we know and live as we encounter the God who has chosen us and called us? It's time to use our imagination. It's time to imagine God's reality! That means it's time for us to experience some attitude adjustment! We must be willing to put aside our comforts, our wants and our needs—we must be willing to step from the fear of the unknown or the safety of the past into the new thing that God desires to do.

The story is told about a young preacher who was pastoring a very traditional and established church. The church was beginning to experience phenomenal growth. It got to the place where the sanctuary was no longer suitable for the congregation. They were going to have to buy or build a new sanctuary. The young preacher had a vision, but she had to come to the church meeting and present her vision to the church. So she came to the meeting ready to share her vision of how God was leading the church to expand their facility. She finished her presentation and waited for a response from the church members that had gathered.

Fairly quickly, a gentleman rose to his feet and said, "Preacher, I thank God for you, but we can't move from this building." The young preacher stood there not knowing what to say. The church member continued, "Pastor, we can't move from this building because that pulpit you preach from—my grandfather used to preach from that pulpit. This chair I just arose from is where my daddy used to pray. And this post that I'm standing next to—I accepted Christ standing right next to this post. Now preacher, I don't mean any harm, but we can't move from this building."

The young preacher stood there, speechless.

While she was gathering her thoughts, an older sainted sister in the rear of the room stood to her feet. She said, "Pastor, I would like to make a motion that we give that brother the post and move on with the plan."

If we are going to imagine God's reality, we have to be in the right place and we have to be of the right mind. We have to come to a place individually and corporately where we allow God to own us—to really own us. God must own our lives, our minds and our spirits. God must own our agendas, our desires, our wants and our needs. God must own the ministry of our churches, the way we do worship, the ministries we provide for children and youth, and the ways in which we reach out to our neighbors who are not yet in the Church. If we are going to imagine and live into the reality of God for us as a Church, we have to get to the place—it is not about us and our reality. Instead, it has to be about God and God's reality. We need to refocus on God's desire and God's plan.

Paul said it to the Romans and we need to hear it as well:

> *And so, dear brothers and sisters, I plead with you to give your bodies to God because of all he has done for you. Let them be a living and holy sacrifice—the kind he will find acceptable. This is truly the way to worship him. Don't copy the behavior and customs of this world, but let God transform you into a new person by changing the way you think. Then you will learn to know God's will for you, which is good and pleasing and perfect.*
>
> *—Romans 12:1-2*

I need to hear and claim this truth over and over again and renew my commitment to apply it within my life. Maybe the same is true for you. If I am going to imagine God's reality and live into God's reality, then I need to get to that place where I fully offer my life to God and allow God to make me who I was created to be. I know what I need to do to make that happen. I'm guessing you know what you need to do to make that happen—most of us do. Let's stop making excuses and let's do it.

When we choose to live in the place where God owns us, when we choose surrender and when we choose God's reality over our reality, we then fully experience the truth of Ephesians 3. We expect God to do what God has promised:

> *God can do anything, you know—far more than you could ever imagine or guess or request in your wildest dreams! He does it not by pushing us around but by working within us, his Spirit deeply and gently within us. Glory to God in the church! Glory to God in the Messiah, in Jesus! Glory down all the generations! Glory through all millennia! Oh, yes!*

—Ephesians 3:20-21

Imagine a Church that knows and shares unimaginable love. Imagine a Church that claims unimaginable power. Imagine a Church that unapologetically engages the mission of making more disciples of Jesus *so* that the world might be changed. Imagine what will be when we truly claim our identity as people of resurrection!

—Bishop Mark Webb

Bishop Mark Webb serves as the episcopal leader for the Upper New York Area, a recent merger of three Annual Conferences in that state. He is a native of Williamsport, PA and holds degrees from Shippensburg University and Asbury Theological Seminary. Prior to his election as a bishop he served pastorates in the Susquehanna Conference and served five years as a district superintendent.

CHAPTER 2

From Road Kill to New Creation

A SEMINARY CLASS in the mission of the Church discussed Paul S. Minear's classic study, *Images of the Church in the New Testament*. Following an overview of dominant and triumphant images depicting the nature and mission of the Church, I asked the students to identify an image that most described their local churches. Images of decline, death, weakness and defeat were prevalent—wilted flowers, headless chicken, crippled bird, beached whale, sinking ship, crumbling building, cracked foundation, etc.

A group of student pastors identified the most striking image. "You've seen road kill, haven't you, Bishop?" remarked one student. "That's my congregation! It is lying on the edge of the road barely quivering with life!" He went on to explain that the congregation had dwindled to less than 20 elderly, infirm persons; numerical growth seemed impossible. Had I taken a vote on which image most characterized the contemporary Church in America, road kill would have won!

Here was a group of 40 young, mostly United Methodist, seminarians preparing for ordained ministry. Yet, their image of the Church is road kill. Those aspiring pastors viewed a Church in decline, run over by societal forces and demographic changes, now "quivering" on the roadside amid rushing traffic. With such an image of the institution to which they were preparing to give their lives, why were these intellectually bright, missionally passionate, theologically inquisitive and idealistic men and women spending thousands of dollars and enduring years of grueling preparation in order to serve road kill?

I asked, "If the Church is road kill, what is the image that characterizes your pastoral ministry?" Are you the driver of the next car now faced with the possibility of putting the poor creature out of its misery, or perhaps swerving to pass it by on your way to the next appointment? Or, are you a veterinarian who will rescue the wounded animal? Or, maybe you see yourself as the highway crew charged with the task of getting the helpless animal out of the traffic! Perhaps you are simply a bystander with fleeting sympathy for a vulnerable creature but no inclination to do more than grieve. Or, you may be a taxidermist who seeks to transform the trembling creature into a lifeless replica of what used to be.

Imagining metaphors matters

Within that vibrant classroom filled with candidates for ministry surfaced key issues confronting The United Methodist Church in North America. Metaphors and images matter! How we imagine the Church and envision ministry are determinative. Much of the conversation in the denomination centers on images of decline and death. Persistent membership loss, dwindling financial resources, and diminished cultural influence contribute to widespread "crisis talk" among bishops, boards and agencies, pastors and other denominational leaders. The denomination is pictured as road kill, a wounded and impotent institution quivering on the edge of a crowded thoroughfare with little or no influence on the traffic or destination of the travelers.

Images of ministry reflecting a road kill perception of the Church abound! Our itinerant system lends itself to treating declining congregations as temporary stopovers on their way to a "real" Church. They drive slowly past the road kill or pause briefly to await an opportunity for genuine ministry. Smaller congregations with limited resources located in rural areas and economically under-resourced communities become steppingstones for upward mobility rather than contexts for vital ministry. Such pastors become hirelings who fleece the sheep rather than shepherds who nurture and lead the sheep into emerging pastures.

Pastors with a road kill image of the Church easily succumb to the devilish image of rescuers who fall victim to a functional atheism. Many revitalization strategies center on developing saviors in the form of young, creative and energetic entrepreneurial leaders who look to business and corporate models for skills to redeem a diminishing institution. Indeed, responding helpfully to a declining institution requires strong leadership skills! But the notion that visioning processes, strategic plans and corporate leadership development schemes will finally redeem the Church ignores or subordinates the real source of renewal—God's action in the life, death and resurrection of Jesus Christ!

Pondering the road kill metaphor in the light of God's nature and mission shaped the seminary classroom discussion for several sessions. What began as images of decline, death and discouragement, ended in signs of hope, renewal and vitality. Confronting death may be the institutional Church's first step toward renewal. It just may lead the Church to its source of life.

Imagining God's response to road kill

The image of road kill sparked a serious theological discussion among the seminary students. "Where is God in relationship to road kill?" I asked the aspiring pastors. God is no stranger to threatened demise and death. In fact, road kill goes to the heart of who God is, where God is, what God is doing and what God calls us to be and do. According to Scripture, God has a special kinship with those quivering on the margins between death and life.

While tending Jethro's sheep, Moses learned who and where God is and what God desires. From the burning bush came this radical declaration from Yahweh: *"I have observed the misery of my people who are in Egypt; I have heard their cry on account of their taskmasters. Indeed, I know their sufferings, and I have come down to deliver them . . ."* (Exodus 3:7-8). The eternal God who creates and sustains all existence sees the wretchedness, hears the faint groans, and feels the anguish of the trembling masses of humanity wounded by forces within and beyond their control. God knows road kill firsthand!

God is revealed in Hebrew Scriptures as One who identifies with and defends "the orphans, widows, and sojourners." Protecting the defenseless, defending the powerless, liberating the captives, restoring the alienated—these are the focus of God's saving presence and action! God liberates the slaves from Egyptian bondage and calls them to be a nation, which embodies God's presence with and justice on behalf of the orphans, widows and strangers. God works to give life to road kill!

The prophets persistently warned the Hebrew people that forsaking the poor, the oppressed and the powerless would result in calamity and even death. God had blessed the Hebrews with freedom so they could be a blessing to the world by embodying God's righteousness and justice. The nation's response to the poor was the test of God's justice. Incorporating the most vulnerable into the community and enabling them to have access to the resources necessary to flourish as beloved children of God was an expression of God's justice and righteousness. When the people practiced God's righteousness and justice, the nation prospered; however, when they forgot the poor and powerless, the nation was in peril. Amos, Hosea, Micah, Isaiah, Jeremiah and Ezekiel called the people to remember that they were once poor and powerless (road kill). Failure to practice justice by welcoming the marginalized to the table of God's abundance threatened the nation's future.

When God chose to dwell among humanity, a young, unmarried teenager gave birth to a vulnerable baby. Forced to leave their home in Nazareth to comply with a governmental taxation policy, Mary and Joseph travelled to a little sleepy town of Bethlehem. The baby was born in a stable, homeless and poor. According to Matthew's Gospel, the Holy Family fled as immigrants into Egypt in order to escape the slaughter of the innocents by a cruel dictator. Jesus grew up in a working-class family, associated with outcasts and sinners and received the outsiders and nobodies. He announced his mission in the words of the ancient prophet:

> *The Spirit of the Lord is upon me*
> *Because he has anointed me*
> *to bring good news to the poor.*
> *He has sent me to proclaim release to the captives*
> *and recovery of sight to the blind,*
> *to let the oppressed go free,*
> *to proclaim the year of the Lord's favor.*
>
> —*Luke 4:18-19*

He went about the marketplaces and hillsides announcing the dawning of a new world, a world of compassion, justice, generosity and joy. He healed the sick, touched the untouchables, fed the hungry, blessed little children, forgave the wayward, comforted the sorrowful, raised the dead and challenged the rich and powerful. He used the story of a despised

Samaritan who aided a quivering wounded man along the road as a model of love for God and neighbor. He affirmed a poor widow's mite as authentic generosity. Jesus paid particular attention to road kill!

Identifying with and defending the powerless challenges the forces that push people to the roadside. Jesus (called Emmanuel meaning "God with us") was charged as a criminal by those in power. He was tried, beaten, scorned, spat upon, whipped, ridiculed, stabbed and executed as a felon, the victim of capital punishment. God entered the world and the world treated him as road kill!

But we know the rest of the story! God raised Jesus Christ from the dead! The resurrection is God's response to road kill. The crucified and risen Christ is the image of the invisible God, the firstborn of all creation (from Colossians 1:15) and in him a new creation has come into being. The last word is not death! It is resurrection! God is forever redeeming, reconciling, and transforming road kill. The risen Christ so closely identifies with the poor, the imprisoned, the homeless and the sick that what is done to them is done to him. And, God uses the weak and vulnerable communities and individuals as means of transforming the world.

The Church is called and empowered to be a visible sign, foretaste and instrument of the new creation wrought in Jesus Christ. As the life of the Hebrew people depended upon their embodiment of God's hospitality and justice toward the orphans, widows and immigrants, so the Church's vitality depends upon its response to those on the margins of society, those whom the world considers road kill.

The call to the margins

Scholars chronicle the demise of Christendom in Western societies and many mourn the loss of the Church's institutional prominence and prestige in America. Within my lifetime, local churches have moved from the center of family and community activity to a weak competitor with sporting events and multiple voluntary organizations. Neighborhood developers once considered the presence of a church a positive marketing asset while, increasingly, congregations face tough zoning restrictions and limitations. Many church facilities constructed when "build it and they will come" was an operative principle now stand nearly vacant and have trouble paying utilities and maintenance costs. Each year, in Conferences in the United States, churches that once thrived are declared abandoned or closed. Many more, like the one served by the student pastor, barely twitch with life as members move away, become frail or die.

While many see the loss of cultural prominence as a threat to the Church, it may be an occasion for reclaiming theological and missional identity. Charles H. Bayer sees the demise of Christendom as an opportunity for "discover[ing] and liv[ing] into a new ecclesial paradigm."[1]

"In this new paradigm," Bayer writes, "the church interprets its cultural and religious marginalization as providential in that it returns the church to the generative site for its mission and ministry: the margins, with and on behalf of the marginalized."[2]

Hendrik Pieterse adds that by turning toward the margins, the Church "can grasp for our day the simple but profound truth . . . the church's healing into faithfulness lies in the company of those despised, marginalized and excluded. . . . "[3]

---

1 Quoted by Hendrik R. Pieterse in a paper delivered at the 2007 Oxford Institute for Theological Studies and published by the General Board of Higher Education and Ministry as a monogram entitled "Opting for the Margins, Again: Why United Methodists Need the Poor to be the Church." The quote is from Charles H. Bayer, *A Resurrected Church: Christianity after the Death of Christendom* (St. Louis: Chalice, 2001)

2 Ibid.

3 Ibid, 3.

Identifying the Church as road kill or as a marginalized institution may be the first step toward resurrection! The margins are the appropriate location of the Church. The Church belongs among society's road kill! The disestablishment of the Church in American society is an opportunity to reclaim an ecclesial identity as a set-apart community in service to the *Missio Dei*, or the "mission of God." As a people bearing the *Imago Dei*, or "the image of God," the Church is only the Church when it owns its identity as an alternative community to the prevailing consumerist culture and joins God on the margins among the vulnerable, poor, abused, powerless and suffering—those whom Jesus called "the least of these" and Charles Wesley referred to as "Jesus' bosom friends."

It is from the margins that the Church bears witness to the God of the Exodus and Jesus; and it is among the oppressed, the imprisoned, the sick, the dying and the pushed aside that the Church is a herald and visible sign, foretaste and instrument of God's new creation. Among those viewed as road kill are the poor; the incarcerated and their families; the frail elderly, especially those with Alzheimer's and other forms of dementia; the immigrants and undocumented workers; and the addicted and abused.

Every community has its marginalized populations that are often "hidden" from view in mobile home parks, jails or prisons, nursing homes, migrant communities and addiction treatment centers. Students in the missiology class were assigned the task of finding the hidden, marginalized people in their communities and engaging them in conversation about faith and the Church. The student pastors who saw their small congregations as road kill with little opportunity for growth protested that there were no hidden people in their communities. Much to their surprise, however, many discovered within easy driving distance seasonal farm workers living in makeshift houses or a state prison surrounded by barbed wire or a mobile home park hidden in the woods. One student discovered that the neighborhood included more than 50 infirm elderly persons who lived alone and had little contact with others.

The final assignment in the mission class was the development of a ministry plan in response to the marginalized populations within their own neighborhoods. The plan had to include the following components: theological/biblical rationale and foundation of the Church's mission, description of the marginalized population, brief history and description of the congregation, the gifts the marginalized have to bring to the congregation, the gifts the congregation can offer the marginalized and the broad outline of a strategy to build relationships of mutual sharing of gifts. In the fulfillment of the assignment, several seminarians found hope and renewed vision and passion for ministry.

From road kill to new creation

Resurrection and new creation are at the core the Christian gospel! God redeems road kill and forges a new creation from what appears as defeat and death. The wounded, bruised, and broken body of Christ has been raised as the firstborn of a new creation. God has won the decisive victory over the powers of sin and death that threaten God's purposes for creation; and the Church can live with hope and courage in the light of the present and coming reign of Christ's kingdom of justice, compassion, generosity and joy. In so doing, new life emerges even amid death!

The future of the Church is not in jeopardy! Prior to 1988 when The United Methodist Hymnal was adopted by General Conference, the liturgy for reception of members included this foundational declaration of the Church's permanence and mission:

The Church is of God and will be preserved to the end of time for the conduct of worship and due administration of the Word and Sacraments, the maintenance of Christian fellowship, the edification of believers, and the conversion of the world. All persons stand in need of the means of grace which it alone supplies.

The declaration of the Church's endurance "to the end of time" is rooted in Jesus' response to Peter's testimony, *"You are the Messiah, the Son of the living God."*

Jesus proclaimed: *"Blessed are you, Simon son of Jonah! For flesh and blood has not revealed this to you, but my Father in heaven. And I tell you, you are Peter, and on this rock I will build my church, and the gates of Hades will not prevail against it"* (Matthew 16:16-18). For centuries, persons preparing for membership in the Church learned that they were being incorporated into an indestructible community preserved, empowered and sent into the world as the "Body of Christ" to embody and to bear witness to God's present and coming reign.

Preoccupation with the survival of the Church in its current form exposes an idolatry that limits the Church to its sociological characteristics. Sociology and anthropology have replaced ecclesiology and theology as the source of the Church's identity, nature and mission. Membership, attendance and financial statistics have become vital life signs just as blood pressure, heart rate and brain waves are measures of human life. Strategic planning processes, leadership formation initiatives and marketing techniques become the primary agency for securing the Church's future rather than presence and power of God at work through the Holy Spirit in the worship, Sacraments, fellowship and proclamation of the Church.

While "the Church will be preserved until the end of time," the institutional expressions of the Body of Christ constantly confront new challenges that require new structures, strategies and actions. However, it is God who raised Jesus Christ from the dead, created the Church at Pentecost and empowers the Church to bear witness to the present and coming reign of Jesus Christ! It is God, therefore, who sustains and renews the Church! Nevertheless, there are actions in every age that prepare the Church for renewal.

Images and actions for a road kill Church

What actions are needed for a disestablished Church—a Church on the margins of a consumerist dominated society—to prepare for renewal? What images of ministry and mission should shape the leaders of congregations similar to the ones the student identified as road kill? The following are offered as suggestive images and actions for nurturing congregations toward renewal as signs and instruments of the new creation wrought in Jesus Christ.

Ministering as foundation–builder and teacher

Methodism began as a renewal movement within an established church that had lost its vitality and relationship with the masses, especially the poor. Although the movement grew from a few Oxford University students in the 1720s to approximately 60,000 at the time of Wesley's death in 1791, the Methodists represented a very small percentage of the population—estimated to be approximately 8 million. What John and Charles Wesley did, however, was lay the foundation for subsequent growth and vitality. They were teachers and pastors who repaired the weakened doctrinal and missional foundation.

Toward the end of his long ministry, John Wesley expressed concern that "the people called Methodists" had lost their zeal and effectiveness. In his sermon, "Causes of the Inefficacy of Christianity," he identifies three losses leading to the inefficacy of Christianity—the loss of doctrine, discipline and self-denial.

Much of his ministry was devoted to clarifying, interpreting and appropriating core Christian doctrines in his context. Through the Wesley brothers' sermons, letters, treatises, hymns and teaching, they reconnected the Methodists to the early Christian affirmations as the lens through which to view the world and the foundation for the formation of Christian character. Class meetings and bands were structures in which the Methodists practiced the means of grace in a community of support and accountability. Visitation of the sick and the incarcerated, medical clinics for the poor, sewing cooperatives, lending agencies and schools were acts of mercy which meant that Methodism was a movement of, for, with and by the poor.

The prevailing consumerism of American society has contributed to identifying the church primarily as a social institution among multiple institutions competing for the loyalties of the people. A consequence of the commodification of culture has been the severing of religious doctrines, language, symbols and practices from their story of origin and meaning. The Church has forgotten "the story" that gave it birth, formed its identity, defined its mission and gave it agency to act in the world. The Church has a profound case of amnesia, and an institution or an individual with amnesia depends on others to define identity and mission. Our identity and mission as the Church are included in the story contained in Scripture, and the liturgies, which are creeds and practices of a long tradition of diverse people in multiple cultural contexts. The biblical stories and creeds and affirmations and liturgies have been ripped from their contexts and complex history of development and now function as ornaments or marketing tools.

Therefore, the practice of Christian ministry today requires that attention be given to teaching understanding and forming communities that reconnect the doctrines, liturgies and practices to the story of God's reign. Or, as Vincent Miller contends, the Church needs to develop tactics of "embedding doctrines, symbols, and practices within their historical tradition and the ongoing life of the community."[4]

Ministry in the 21st century must focus on repairing and rebuilding the foundations upon which ministry is built. Foundation work is basic, unglamorous and subterranean. Consumerism with its accompanying Church growth strategies, structures and modalities has won the day in this generation. We have an ever-growing number of structures and strategies built on foundations of sand. What is necessary is laying a solid foundation for potential renewal, much as the Wesleys did in the 18th century.

More is required than mastering orthodox doctrine, creeds and theological affirmations. Interpreting those doctrines in the contemporary world requires exegeting social contexts as skillfully as exegeting sacred texts! Here our United Methodist "Doctrinal Standards and our Theological Task" is helpful.[5]

Teaching requires knowing the basic doctrines that the Church has agreed upon and that form the primary lens through which we view reality and provide the mooring, from which we launch our theological explorations. Those must be communicated, interpreted and appropriated in diverse contexts. Therefore, theological exploration is necessary! Theologies provide lenses and tools for understanding and interpreting and communicating the story of God's mission in the world. Such theological knowledge and insight must be connected with the realities existing in local neighborhoods and the global village.

---

4 Vincent J. Miller, *Consuming Religion: Christian Faith and Practice in a Consumerist Culture* (New York: Continuum International Publishing Group Inc., 2005), p. 194

5 *Book of Discipline, The United Methodist Church 2004*, Part II, "Doctrinal Standards and Our Theological Task". For my own interpretation and commentary on the doctrinal statement, see *Who Are We? Doctrine, Ministry, and Mission of The United Methodist Church, Leader's Guide* (Nashville: The United Methodist Publishing House), 2001 Revised edition.

During my years as a bishop, I grieved the closing of churches that were surrounded by people. The demographics of the neighborhoods changed and the churches remained isolated from and even contemptuous of their new neighbors. Many of those churches had seminary-trained pastors. They used all the right curriculum resources, even engaged in quality liturgical practices. But they didn't connect to their communities. They recited the creeds, sang the hymns, even studied the denomination's beliefs; but they failed to live the creeds in the local context.

A pastor was appointed to an inner-city congregation that had once thrived as a neighborhood church. As the demographics changed and members moved to the surrounding suburbs, the church had dwindled to a few elderly constituents. The once majestic building located on several acres of vacant land began to deteriorate and the congregation moved into the small chapel. Young families with children moved into the rental houses surrounding the church building. A public housing unit a few blocks away housed scores of the working poor. It was a road kill congregation!

"What is your image of ministry in this place?" the district superintendent asked the newly appointed pastor.

She replied, "A lot of foundation work has to be done and I'm not talking just about the building. I've got to do a lot of teaching which will help us live 'the Jesus story' in this neighborhood."

There followed a year of intense study/teaching of the story of God's mighty acts of salvation as revealed in Scripture and supremely in the life, teaching, death and resurrection of Jesus Christ. Running through the studies and discussions was this question: What does it mean to live God's story in this community? Dramatic changes began to take place. An Alcoholics Anonymous group began meeting in the facilities. A support group for formerly incarcerated persons was initiated. Neighborhood children began to play on the church property. After an extensive survey and assessment in the community, it was determined that adequate affordable housing was a pressing need. The congregation made a radical and risky decision! They decided to give up their parsonage and vacate the land for the building of houses for low-income families. Partnerships were formed with Habitat for Humanity and the churches of the district to build five houses. The houses were completed within three months and a service of celebration planned. The new homeowner families, workers on the houses, people from the neighborhood and district churches filled the sanctuary for an evening of praise and thanksgiving. Following the service, a meal provided by a large suburban congregation drew together the motley group of suburbanites and residents of public housing, neighborhood kids and the elderly members of the congregation. New creation emerged from road kill and the foundation was laid for continuing to live the Jesus story.

Ministering as a witness to God's reign

At the heart of the Jesus story is the good news of the present and coming reign of God. The Gospel of Mark inaugurates Jesus's ministry in these words, *"Now after John was arrested, Jesus came to Galilee, proclaiming the good news of God, and saying, 'The time is fulfilled, and the kingdom of God has come near; repent, and believe in the good news.'"* The reign of God's justice, compassion, generosity and hope was present in Jesus Christ and wherever he went the kingdom was present! He pointed to signs of God's reign and invited people to live now in the light of the future God is forever bringing.

In the cross of Jesus Christ, God engaged the principalities and powers that threaten God's reign of justice, compassion, generosity and hope. In the resurrection, God delivered an eternal *"yes"* to everything Jesus said and did and a decisive *"no"* to all that attempts to defeat God's vision and goal for creation. Indeed, the Risen Christ is the firstborn of God's new creation and the image of the future God is bringing. As the apostle Paul declares:

> He [Christ] is the image of the invisible God, the firstborn of all creation; . . . For in him all the fullness of God was pleased to dwell, and through him God was pleased to reconcile to himself all things, whether on earth or in heaven, by making peace through the blood of the cross.

—*Colossians 1:15-20*

God in Jesus Christ is bringing into existence a reconciled and transformed creation. The eschatological vision of God's final victory provides the content and energy for the Church's mission. What is God's dream for the world? What will the new creation look like when God's victory is complete? The Bible and our basic Christian doctrines provide the basic characteristics of God's vision toward which the Church is called to live and by which its faithfulness is judged.

Among the signs of God's reign in Jesus Christ are these:

- All creation will be healed, from the scarred majestic hilltops to the polluted mountain streams, from the punctured ozone to the diseased human cell, from the chaotic forces of nature to the confused human mind.
- A people will know their identity as beloved children of God, made in the divine image and redeemed in Jesus Christ, with infinite worth and dignity.
- The human family will be one, with all barriers of race, class, gender, religion, politics, and sexual orientation removed, and all violence and exploitation and cruelty ended.
- Justice and righteousness will permeate the whole creation, with the least and most vulnerable having access to the table of God's abundance and all will

have everything necessary to flourish as integral components of God's creation.

This is the new world brought near in Jesus Christ. It is the world for which we long when we pray, "Thy kingdom come, thy will be done on earth as it is in heaven." These are the vital signs of congregational life! Jesus called attention to the presence of the new creation in the midst of the old world. He invited the disciples to live now in God's new world and to bear witness to God's reign. Jesus was asked by the Pharisees when the kingdom of God was coming, and he answered, "*The kingdom of God is not coming with things that can be observed; nor will they say, 'Look, here it is!' or 'There it is!' For, in fact, the kingdom of God is among you*" (Luke 17:20-21).

The Church is called to be a witness, sign, foretaste and instrument of this new creation. Awareness of the presence of God's reign in Christ provides energy for the Church's mission. During my years as an active bishop, I often opened cabinet meetings with the question: "Where have you seen the presence and power of God at work since we last met?" Rather than beginning with problems and conflicts to be resolved, we began with signs of God's reign in the midst of local congregations and communities. We specifically asked for examples of the healing of creation, persons experiencing their identity as beloved children of God, barriers being overcome and justice advancing. The energy level of the cabinet increased and we addressed the problems with hope and confidence.

Students in the seminary mission class were asked to reflect on the same question as they visited the people on the margins in their communities. They were cautioned to avoid the notion that they were "taking God to the margins;" rather, they were to assume that God was already present and working among the hidden people in their neighborhoods. As Wesleyans, we trust that God's prevenient grace goes before us and is at work within and among all people. The responses both from cabinet members and students reminded me of this passage in Luke: *"The seventy returned with joy, saying, 'Lord, in your name even the demons submit to us!'"* (Luke 10:17).

Focus on membership decline and diminished institutional prominence depletes the Church's energy and presumes a theology of scarcity rather than confidence born in resurrection. Where God's righteousness is present, there is always enough! Furthermore, preoccupation with institutional survival diverts attention away from the present and coming reign of God, the penultimate (the institutional Church) replaces the ultimate (God's present and coming reign in Christ). The Church turns in on itself rather than outward toward what God is doing in the world!

The Church is called to bear witness to the vision of God's ultimate victory and to point to signs of its presence in the world, including our neighborhoods. A small congregation located in a small town in the Mississippi Delta faced almost certain death. The membership had been reduced to a few elderly white landowners. The congregation could not support a full-time pastor and could barely pay utilities and maintenance cost. An enthusiastic retired elder, who was known as a storyteller, was appointed as pastor. He had a particular gift of connecting with diverse people and honoring the image of God in all people.

The largest employers in the county were the nearby casinos, which attracted visitors from all over the country. The pastor, though opposed to gambling, considered the casinos and the employees and visitors as part of his parish. He visited with workers and patrons and made an appointment with the managers. He told those who ran the establishments that he strongly disagreed with their business and felt that they exploited people for profits. However, he added that he wasn't there to preach to them but to express concern for the workers and their families, especially the children.

He became an unofficial "chaplain," or pastor, in the casinos, where he gained the trust of food service workers, housekeepers and maintenance personnel as well as the managers and owners. From his conversations, he learned that childcare was a major concern for workers and their families. Conversations and collaboration among church members, parents, casino managers and other partners resulted in establishment of a childcare center at the church. With the assistance of many people and diverse agencies, the facilities were renovated and appropriately equipped. Grants and gifts made possible trained teachers and aids. Volunteers from the congregation and community supplemented the paid staff. Soon, the mostly vacant building was filled with black and brown and white children playing and learning together. Gradually, children and their parents from the casinos began attending worship services. There, in delta flatlands amid a racially and class-segregated community and the neon glitter of a questionable industry, a small congregation, barely quivering with life, became a visible sign and instrument of God's new creation. Children owned a new identity as beloved children of God. Barriers of race, economics and class crumbled. Dim signs of justice appeared! Road kill experienced resurrection!

Ministering as networker and partner

The conviction that God's preoccupation is the salvation of the cosmos broadens the Church's vision and expands its practice of mission. God's mission includes the healing and transformation of the entire cosmos, including human hearts, communities, nations and the created order. Identifying where God is at work in the world and commitment to participate in the divine mission enables the Church to discover partners and coworkers in God's mission.

While God has called the Church to be a visible witness and instrument of the new creation, God's presence and work in the world is not limited to the institutional Church. Wherever healing, justice, reconciliation and wholeness are taking place, God in Christ through the Holy Spirit is at work! Therefore, a major challenge of mission today is identifying partners and building relationships of mutual trust, learning and transformation.

Concentration on institutional triumphalism often leads to competitiveness and conflict rather than cooperation and connection. Jesus confronted the shortsightedness of the disciples when they tried to stop a man from casting out demons who "does not follow with us." Jesus cautioned the disciples, *"Do not stop him; for whoever is not against you is for you"* (Luke 9:49-50).

When the goal is bearing witness to God's reign of justice, healing, reconciliation and peace, the Church finds partners in unexpected places. Bearing witness also avoids the temptation of paternalism that robs people of their dignity as beloved children of God and fails to acknowledge and receive the gifts of those on the margins. Rather than relating to those on the margins as "projects," they become friends and a means of grace in our transformation.

Networking has become a common strategy in every realm of the modern world. It is made possible by the advances in technologies that connect individuals, nations, institutions and governments around the world. The world has indeed become a "global village"! Relationships are formed across geographical, cultural, national and religious boundaries. The Internet connects people around the world and enables the forming of heretofore-impossible relationships of mutual sharing.

The pastor in the Mississippi Delta saw the entire county as part of his parish and the context of God's mission. He went to the margins and formed relationships with diverse members of the community. In so doing, he discovered and brought together needs and gifts that enabled a declining congregation to be a catalyst of justice, reconciliation and healing. What he did in a local community is possible across geographic boundaries.

Methodism offers ready-made opportunities for networking! Connection is part of our DNA! Through Annual

Conferences, the General Board of Global Ministries, Volunteers in Mission, Pan Methodist Campaign for Children in Poverty and numerous ecumenical and nonprofit agencies, thousands of local churches are networking with people across the globe to become signs and instruments of God's new creation. Good news is being brought to the poor, release to captives and sight to the blind. Barriers of race and nation and language are being dismantled. Justice is being advocated for the immigrants, the oppressed, the suffering and the powerless!

Conclusion

The discussion of road kill in the seminary classroom sparked intense theological, missional and pastoral reflection and imagination. Several of the students are now serving local congregations. Others are in ministry as prison and hospital chaplains, community organizers, social workers and teachers. I have kept in touch with several and the following are some signs of resurrection in their ministries:

- The student who coined the road kill image formed a relationship with the juvenile court in his community and involved his congregation in ministry with troubled youth.
- One who entered seminary after a career in business is now recruiting and training volunteers from local churches to lead Disciple Bible Study in prisons and incorporate ex-offenders in the Church's fellowship and ministry.
- Another serves as an associate pastor in a large church with the specific responsibility for connecting the congregation to the local and global community and she regularly connects the local church to individuals and communities in Africa.

- Another former student started a church among the poor in a large urban area and connects resources from the Annual Conference, local congregations and community to enable a holistic ministry among very diverse people.
- Among the additional signs of resurrection are congregations forming relationships with undocumented workers, families of incarcerated men and women, frail elderly and those suffering from dementia.

These and countless other committed clergy and laity are repairing theological and missional foundations through teaching and embedding the story of God's mighty acts of salvation, forming relationships of mutual friendship with the hidden marginalized people in their communities and networking with other congregations and agencies in being witnesses, signs and instruments of resurrection! Across the world, road kill is being resurrected!

—*Bishop Kenneth L. Carder*

Bishop Kenneth Carder is the Ruth W. and A. Morris Williams professor emeritus of the Practice of Christian Ministry at Duke Divinity School and currently serves as the senior visiting professor of Wesley Studies at Lutheran Theological Southern Seminary in Columbia, SC. He was elected to the episcopacy in 1992 and retired in 2004. He is the author of five books and numerous articles.

CHAPTER 3

Finding Hope in Our Mission

THE UNITED METHODIST Church has transformed my life in ways I could never have anticipated. I thank God every-day for the Church's existence. One profound experience with the Church has shaped every fiber of who I am, and I want to share this story with you.

My parents made a commitment very early in my life that we would be raised in a Christian Church, and they happened to start attending the Wesley United Methodist Church in San Jose when I was only 5 years old. They started by dropping my sister and myself off for Sunday school each week, but soon they decided to get involved themselves. It was a life-changing decision for our family.

My dad was always self-employed, and my mom was a classic 1960s stay-at-home mom. June Cleaver or Claire Hux-table had nothing on my mom. My mom would iron our socks; she ironed our underwear; she ironed our bed sheets—changed once a week, with hospital corners. In fact, everyday she would make our beds and fluff up the pillows like a hotel service. There was not a speck of dust in the house. Every evening there would be a home-cooked dinner from scratch with a homemade dessert. She was the center of our household, and we were a very close family. When I was 14 years old, my mom was diagnosed with cancer, and after a short but valiant fight, we lost her before Christmas. It was if the bottom fell out of our whole family—she was so central to our lives.

After she died, each one of us had a steady stream of friends and family who stayed with us leading up to the funeral service. It was then that I noticed that the friends who came the most and stayed the longest were our church friends. Most of all, the church was there for us, providing care and comfort in our desperate time of need. The funeral service was going to be hard, but our pastor, the Rev. Wes Yamaka, provided hope and assurance that it was a wonderful tribute to her life and ours. The sanctuary filled. Then, the basement filled, and they started putting folks into the classrooms, which were in a separate building. This was before audio and video feeds, so some of these folks sat through the whole service not hearing or seeing anything.

When I got out of the service, we were to travel in a funeral procession to the cemetery for the burial. The cars were lined up waiting for us to lead, and I remember looking at the waiting cars. I literally could not see the end of the line! I then realized what the Church of Jesus Christ meant to me. With all of these people who loved my mom and our family offering their support and care, how could we not survive? How could we not make it? And we did! We did. This experience symbolized all that is good and life-affirming about the Church of Jesus Christ. My loyalty to The United Methodist Church would never falter. This was The United Methodist Church transforming lives—transforming my life! It set the stage for my own journey of faith, and even though I had many options for a professional career, it is why I chose Christian ministry in the end.

Such profound experiences in Christian discipleship also shaped the ethos and direction of my own life. I have been transformed through the power of God in Jesus Christ through the Holy Spirit, and this means that I must work for the greater transformation of the world by making that world a better place. As I love God and neighbor as myself, there is a call placed on my life. By myself, my capacity to affect change is limited. When we work in Christian community, our outcome is magnified as we join others in a common purpose. Together, transformation becomes possible.

A biblical foundation for our mission: Isaiah 43:14-21

Thus says the Lord, your Redeemer, the Holy One of Israel: For your sake I will send to Babylon and break down all the bars, and the shouting of the Chaldeans will be turned to lamentation. I am the Lord, your Holy One, the Creator of Israel, your King.

Thus says the Lord, who makes a way in the sea, and a path in the mighty waters, who brings out chariot and horse, army and warrior; they lie down, they cannot rise, they are extinguished, quenched like a wick:

Do not remember the former things, or consider the things of old. I am about to do a new thing; now it springs forth, do you not perceive it? I will make a way in the wilderness and rivers in the desert. The wild animals will honor me, the jackals and the ostriches; for I give water in the wilderness, rivers in the desert, to give drink to my chosen people, the people whom I formed for myself so that they might declare my praise.

Throughout history, countless people have been inspired by these words from Second Isaiah. Probably written in Babylon, the prophet is dealing with the depression and hopelessness of the people in exile; the people are yearning for some positive message from God.

Undoubtedly, the prophet is attempting to counter the lamentations and fear of the people, who have found themselves in a dire situation. It is something universal about the people of God: When things are not going well, we complain. This is relevant to our present time as churches that are fighting to survive and facing dwindling resources complain often and loudly to anyone who will hear. When we find ourselves complaining, we would do well to remember God's suggested course of action in verse 21 of this Scripture: *"So that they might declare my praise."* Even when things are not going well, we should praise God.

Isaiah 43:14 promises what the exiles desire most: God's immediate presence and intervention. They are desperate for salvation and freedom and they trust that the Holy One who created Israel will not forsake them. However, we know from history that their final salvation and freedom will take decade upon decade. A whole generation will pass away before God liberates the people from exile. We need to be reminded of this historical fact in light of the promises that are made in this and other prophetic passages.

References to the Exodus in verses 16-17 should buoy the people's hope: God intervened to save their ancestors and drowned the military in the Red Sea. Instead, however, the prophet proclaims that they are *"not to remember the former things, or consider the things of old."* This is a sobering message, since we know that God will not liberate them for another 70 years. God's promises are always under God's conditions and timeline, not ours.

The central crux of this passage is found in verse 18, with God's promise: *"I am about to do a new thing; now it springs forth, do you not perceive it?"* The people may expect God to take action like in the past, but the prophet reminds them that God is doing something different. The new way will not be liberation through the Red Sea, as before, but through the wilderness itself. God promises that rivers will run through the desert, providing what is necessary for the people to survive. This action may not be what the people are expecting or hoping for, but God's desire is that the people will praise their Creator in all circumstances.

As the Creator, it is God's radical prerogative to be who God will be. The right order here is all-important: God does not exist for us. Rather, we exist for God. God is always doing something new, and it is God, not us, who defines what that is. We may not "like" God's new thing, and we may even be disappointed by it at first—but God will certainly create something new. In God's infinite wisdom that new thing will always be for the betterment of all creation.

We can always count on something new from God. I firmly believe that God is creating something new for the Church of Jesus Christ, even though none of us can yet envision what that new thing will be. I feel it deeply in my soul that the Holy Spirit is moving us to something new. I am less sure about the institutional Church that we know, for manifestations of the Church of Jesus Christ wax and wane—it is not that important which denominations survive in their current form. I know that the Church of Jesus Christ will never die, and even now, God is doing a new thing for that Church.

Do you not perceive it?

The mission of The United Methodist Church

The current mission statement of the United Methodist Church reads: "The mission of the church is to make disciples of Jesus Christ for transformation of the world."

Prior to the year 2000, our Church operated without a central mission statement. I believe it created somewhat of a void in our collective ministry. The first official iteration of our mission statement simply read: "The mission of the church is to make disciples of Jesus Christ."

An explanatory sentence followed this simple statement: "Local churches provide the most significant arena through which disciple-making occurs."

It was primarily the Council of Bishops who felt that this mission statement, while accurate, did not fully express the theological rationale for our collective purpose. Something was missing in this original sentence. Namely, for what purpose do we make disciples of Jesus Christ?

Our founder, John Wesley, believed that the culmination of our discipleship would lead to the state of entire sanctification or perfection in Christ. In this divine state, our love of God and neighbor would eclipse our own self-interested nature. Thus, we would become the "new creature" in Christ Jesus that the apostle Paul envisioned. Wesley also believed that the Scriptures revealed a future where all of creation would be transformed into this newness. From the book of Revelation, Wesley believed we were promised a world where *"Death will be no more; mourning and crying and pain will be no more, for the first things have passed away"* (Revelation 21: 4b).

Thus, many bishops and UMC leaders started using the phrase "for the transformation of the world" as an addition to the original mission statement. The people claimed the words as their own in 2008, when the General Conference overwhelmingly accepted our current mission statement in the present form.

I feel that this is a rock-solid mission statement, although it has some detractors who believe it should be updated anew. Some of us have been toying with the transposition of the wording, and Bishop Roy Sano has suggested the following: "For the transformation of the world, we are to make disciples of Jesus Christ."

One of Bishop Sano's rationales for this transposition mirrors his own faith journey. We are compelled by the goal of transforming the world and come into discipleship to Jesus Christ because of this purpose. I think this sentiment speaks volumes to the post-boomer generations. Many young people are not interested in organized religion at all, but they feel compelled to make a difference in the world. As one young person I know put it: "I want to transform the world, that is for sure, but I'm just not sure about this Jesus Christ stuff ... "

Mission can be a gateway to meeting Christ. When participating in the mission projects that our Church sponsors to transform the world, many people get hooked into a discipleship paradigm. People who might be reluctant to join their Christian friends in worship will often gladly join them in mission. If we do not have a concrete strategy to make disciples of Jesus Christ in our missionary endeavors, we are missing the boat in our evangelism.

It's important to pair the "micro-level" work of making disciples with the "macro-level" work of transformation of the world. Intuitively, we know that making disciples of Jesus Christ happens mainly at the micro level of personal relationships—local churches are the most significant arenas where this takes place. Conversely, large-scale transformation of the world takes place primarily at the macro level—if 12 million United Methodists decide to do something together, worldwide change will certainly take place. The combination of micro-level efforts (making disciples of Jesus Christ) paired with the macro-level (for the transformation of the world) provide a holistic approach that makes our United Methodist Church great.

Making disciples of Jesus Christ ...

The core purpose of this book is to celebrate what is good and right about our United Methodist Church. That is easy to do because I see such positives on a daily basis. As a UMC bishop, my role is to see things at the 20,000-foot level—to see the big picture and help the Church focus its mission. At the same time, I must have "boots on the ground" and understand the context that our clergy and laity are dealing with on a daily basis.

Most of us in the UMC are compelled to create vital congregations as we seek renewal and revitalization of our local churches. We share in John Wesley's vision to "spread scriptural holiness" throughout the land. We honestly seek to make new disciples of Jesus Christ on a daily basis. Like many annual conferences, we here in the Greater Northwest Area (the Alaska, Oregon-Idaho, and Pacific Northwest Annual Conferences) have an ambitious goal to plant 50 new faith communities in our area in this quadrennium. However, we realize that just planting new faith communities will not be enough to stem the tide of our membership losses. We are a "graying denomination," in that the average age of our membership is around 58 years old. We have a 15 to 20 year window to make our Church younger, more diverse and more numerically strong.

Coupled with planting new faith communities, we also must revitalize our existing congregations by enabling them to reach younger and more diverse people while making more disciples of Jesus Christ. We are experimenting on many fronts towards this goal. In the following story, I highlight one bright success we have had in our area that exemplifies many of these factors.

Doing something new

On the eastern side of the state of Washington, we have many rural towns that are undergoing tremendous changes in demographics and economics. The agricultural industry has changed remarkably over the years, and the small family farms have largely disappeared. Many of these towns have attracted large Hispanic populations, and our churches have not kept up with either the demographic or economic changes. In the city of Pasco, WA we had a local church that was historically

Anglo in composition. Through the years, the area around the church became largely Hispanic, and the church dwindled in numbers to the point of closure.

A Hispanic congregation was allowed to use the building. They had a fairly strong youth ministry at the time run by Alex and Sally Perez. When the district and Annual Conference took over the building, we immediately saw the opportunity to do a new church plant in the existing building with a Hispanic congregation. This young couple possessed the entrepreneurial gifts to start a new congregation, however, they did not have a long or strong United Methodist background, and our polity and governance system was brand new to them.

The Perezes both had successful careers outside the Church. When we approached them about going into ministry full time, it was quite a discernment struggle. To give up well-paying secular jobs to enter into ministry was both daunting and risky, and would take a real leap of faith for them to do so.

Taking them to the Annual Conference was also taking a risk. Although the Perezes were doing good ministry, they had no formal seminary training. Additionally, in order to give a new church the best opportunity to take hold, the Conference would have to commit two full-time salaries from Board of Congregational Development funding.

However, God is always so good. The Perezes were willing to quit their current jobs and move forward into ministry with us at that location. We had to break some rules, as we had to fast track them into candidacy for ministry so that their work could begin immediately. They proved every bit as successful as we thought they would be. With their charisma and God-given gifts, they were able to immediately build a congregation.

It is one of the most successful new church starts we have had, and they are now outgrowing their building because the size of their congregation continues to increase. They do not have enough parking and small group space as they continue to grow. They started a radio ministry, which has morphed into a television ministry for the whole area. They are now local pastors and are completing our educational requirements through the Course of Study. They are serving in key leadership roles for the Annual Conference, and they have the leadership abilities to replicate their ministry in other small towns and local churches throughout the area.

The Perezes are bright stars for us, and we thank God for sending them our way! It is a success story that has no recent parallel in our area, and it provides an inspiration for us to continue to start new, diverse faith communities.

Learning from success

The first thing we can learn is that revitalization must take seriously the social and demographic context of where the local church finds itself. When the demographics change around a local church, the church must address those changes in a proactive and healthy way. The usual way is for us to ignore those neighborhood changes and hold onto an old DNA that refuses to open the doors to welcome new neighbors. Too often, churches resist demographic diversity until it is too late to revitalize the existing congregation.

We must embrace the diversity we find in our communities. In our Pacific Northwest Annual Conference, the first priority after a church closes is for the Annual Conference and district to offer that ministry to an ethnic community that reflects the neighborhood of the local setting as a possible restart. In other words, our first priority to a closed local church is to investigate the possibility of a neighborhood ministry restart. This commitment to the local mission field is a central part of the DNA of the Annual Conference and reflects our commitment to racial-ethnic diversity.

Second, what we gather from the story of Alex and Sally Perez is that revitalization is all about leadership. It takes both committed leadership in the district and Annual Conference as well as onsite leadership in the local community. There is nothing new in this realization about leadership. However, the finding, nurturing and cultivation of good leadership means taking some risks and thinking outside the box. It is painfully clear to us that we do not have enough indigenous leadership for every local church revitalization or new church plant that we need to create. So we must try new ways of finding and nurturing the leadership that we need.

And third, we must understand that we cannot allow our existing bureaucracy and rules to dictate where the Holy Spirit is leading us. So often, our rules get in the way of us embracing God's new thing from Isaiah, so we have to have courage to break a few rules and take necessary chances in order for new ministry to take root.

The late Peter Drucker used to hammer this concept home repeatedly: "Bureaucracy," in the pejorative sense, "is when the rules become more important than the mission." Our *Book of Discipline* has served us well in the past when the Church needed its management tools to oversee a large and complex organization. However, the world has changed so much around the Church of today. Too often, the *Book of Discipline* makes the rules more important than the mission. Our mission of "making disciples of Jesus Christ for the transformation of the world" must trump even the *Book of Discipline* if we are to be faithful to God's calling.

… for the transformation of the world

Overall, while disciples are made primarily at the local church level, transformation of the world can best be facilitated at the larger denominational level. Our UMC has been at the forefront of huge societal accomplishments. Think of the major institutions that the Methodists have started—universities such as Emory in Atlanta, Southern Methodist in Dallas and Boston University. Our Methodist ancestors have created major hospitals and medical centers across the country. We have also been instrumental in the starting of major movements and enduring institutions like the Salvation Army.

Even in my own lifetime, I have witnessed the UMC's commitment to the transformation of the world. As a young pastor serving on the Board of Higher Education and Ministry, I witnessed the creation of a first-rate university for the entire continent of Africa. On the site of the Old Mutare Mission, we built Africa University from the ground up. It took the commitment of all of us United Methodists in the form of our apportionment giving to create and sustain Africa University. (To see that whole history from an eyewitness account, read Angella Current Felder's book, *The School of Dreams In the Valley of Hope: The Africa University Story*.)

Imagine No Malaria

Our latest UMC project to transform the world comes in our commitment to end malaria related deaths in the continent of Africa. We have committed to raise $75 million to support this goal. The United Methodist Church has never raised this much money for any one single issue in its history, but we are well on our way with over $58 million pledged and collected at the time of this writing.

Our fight against malaria began at the 2008 General Conference. Bishop Thomas Bickerton challenged the delegates to pledge their lunch money to "Nothing But Nets" in honor of World Malaria Day. A donation of only $10 to this organization would purchase a treated bed net to keep those sleeping under it safe from the mosquitoes that spread malaria. The 992 delegates raised $15,000 for the cause, and an auction of a signed basketball by United Methodist bishops raised an additional $429,270 during the conference. To further our fight against malaria, we joined the United Nations Foundation and partnered with UNICEF, the International Red Cross and Nets for Life in net distribution and anti-malaria education.

Since 2010, Nothing But Nets has morphed into what we now call "Imagine No Malaria." Currently, more than two-thirds of all the U.S. Annual Conferences have committed to some formal fundraising on behalf of Imagine No Malaria. Deaths from malaria have already been cut in half! One person used to die from malaria every 30 seconds, and we have seen a decrease to one person every 60 seconds. Unfortunately, the majority of these deaths are children under the age of 5 and pregnant women. This is a disease that can be prevented. The Church must not stop until no one dies from this disease!

Connected in mission

It is important to realize the interconnectedness of transforming the world and making disciples of Jesus Christ. We have been doing great work in Africa by setting up delivery systems of bed nets and enabling an infrastructure to develop around health care. Our United Methodist Church, working through agencies like the United Methodist Committee on Relief (UMCOR), has developed key trusting relationships and physical distribution networks that are critical to the future of Africa. Often, the first step in UMC strategy is to open up a health clinic in a village area and distribute bed nets. Only after these lifesaving things have been provided do we follow with a disciple-making system like a church.

Bishop John Yambasu of the Sierra Leone Episcopal Area told the story of how some local village chiefs came to his office one day and asked him to start churches in their villages. Bishop Yambasu realized that some of these chiefs weren't even Christian, so he asked why they wanted him to start United Methodist Churches in their village. They responded: "We have trusted you with our bodies through the distribution of bed nets and fighting malaria, now we are ready to trust you with our souls."

What a powerful story of the interconnectedness of our mission statement! In transformation of the world, we literally transform lives through faith in Jesus Christ. It is the transformational way we follow in John Wesley's injunction to "spread Scriptural Holiness throughout the land."

We cannot do all that we do in transforming the world as solitary individuals. In working toward raising $75 million to end malaria in Sub-Saharan Africa, there are a few individual and large church gifts over a million dollars. However, the vast majority of our fundraising has come from the grass roots of our denomination. It is the youth car washes, bake sales and community dinners that have contributed to this goal. We are successful because so many United Methodists are working as one. No one individual can end malaria. But, if we work together in Christ, we can do magnificent things that no one else can imagine.

Moments of hope

Amidst the difficulties The United Methodist Church faces in the present time, there are shining moments of hope that emerge to restore our faith. Some of these moments come in the form of unexpected successes, or in small revelatory moments of faith. Some moments of hope come in a breakthrough on a problem or in the simple act of making a positive change. Some of these moments come in the form of people whom God sends to uplift or restore us.

One of my recent moments of faith comes directly through another person. That person was Bishop Jack M. Tuell, whom we recently lost at the joyous age of 90. As a young pastor, I served under Bishop Tuell's appointment in the California-Pacific Annual Conference. Much more recently, he became my mentor and friend. When I was assigned to the Pacific Northwest and Alaska Annual Conferences, Bishop Jack and Marji Tuell were living in the Wesley Homes Terrace in retirement. Their apartment overlooked our Pacific Northwest Annual Conference building. Jack used to kid me that he knew when I was in town because he could see the lights on in my office, and my car parked in the driveway. I thought he was just kidding me, until one day he called me. He said, "Grant, your car lights are on; I thought you'd want to know to turn them off!"

The fact that Jack was actually looking after me was one of the great gifts that God has given me. Beyond making sure my car lights were turned off, he was also watching over me in a spiritual sense. As a rookie bishop, I would consult him whenever I had a difficult problem because he was so close at hand.

Jack's death leaves a great void in my own life, but his wisdom and insight, shared so graciously with me these past 5 years, continue to inspire and motivate me. One of Jack's greatest gifts was that he always looked at the Church with optimism: He was constantly hoping for positive change. He deeply understood the problems our Church is facing, but he also trusted steadfastly in God. In Isaiah 43:19, God promises, *"I am about to do a new thing"* and Jack believed that God's new thing could break forth at any moment. He believed wholeheartedly in the Church of Jesus Christ, and nothing could deter him from his belief in the work and future of God's Church.

As one of the giants of our United Methodist Church Episcopal leadership, Jack was a hero in so many ways for the Church. He literally saved the California-Pacific Annual Conference from bankruptcy during the Pacific Homes crisis and provided a win-win for both the homes and the church. He navigated a settlement that saved Pacific Homes and eventually returned millions of dollars back to the Church both locally and nationally.

And yet, with all of his accomplishments, Bishop Tuell was as humble and self-depreciating as they come. One of his favorite stories was when he and Marji encountered a Church actor who would go around and perform as Charles Wesley. They met him at a church, and Marji introduced herself as someone who knew a thing or two about UMC hymns. Upon hearing the name, he said, "Are you the spouse of the 'Great Jack Tuell?'"

Jack was standing right there and amused at that response, came forward and said, "I'm the Great Jack Tuell."

He would tell that story with a wink as if to say, who would say such a thing? But to many of us, he really was the Great Jack Tuell.

The United Methodist Church is in a dire state, and we need leaders like Jack who dare to hope for our future. Toward the end of his autobiography, *From Law to Grace*, Jack comments on how easy it is to become discouraged over the state of the world. He questions whether we are entering a new Dark Age. His answer comes from his own faith:

> *But, Marji always says that I am an incurable optimist, and this is true. So how is it possible to be optimistic in the face of the forces which seem to be pushing us back to a new Dark Age? For me, the answer has to lie in the realm of religious faith. I believe in God—A God whose very nature has been revealed to us in Jesus Christ. It is clearly the will and intent of God that all of us made in His image should live together in love, peace and justice. That this goal is intended for this world is utterly shown in the prayer Jesus taught us, and which Christians everywhere pray each week: "Thy Kingdom come on earth as it is in heaven." So as a Christian, I am bound to be an optimist—it is God's will that the human community live together in peace and justice—and God's will shall one day be accomplished. (pp. 155-156)*

Being one of those whom Jack touched with the imprint of God, my life has been made better. The spiral continues as I attempt to touch others toward the greater good. If each person reaches out to those near them, like Jack, and unites in the common goal of transforming the world, there is certainly hope for the Body of Christ.

Bishop Jack M. Tuell represents that which is good and right about our United Methodist Church. I dedicate this chapter to him.

—Bishop Grant Hagiya

Bishop Grant Hagiya is the resident bishop of the new Greater Northwest Area which includes the Alaska, Oregon-Idaho and Pacific Northwest Annual Conferences. He graduated with a doctorate in education from Pepperdine University, and a Master of Divinity from Claremont School of Theology. In 2013 he published his first book entitled "Leadership Kaizen: How to Become a Better Church Leader."

CHAPTER 4

Moving Into New Territory

A note from the editor: Bishop Alsted serves the Nordic and Baltic Episcopal Area of The United Methodist Church. This area includes the Nordic countries of Denmark, Finland, Sweden and Norway, and the three Baltic states of Estonia, Latvia and Lithuania. This is an area where Methodism was firmly planted more than 100 years ago and throughout its life has been a minority religion in countries that have had a state church and places where the witness of the Church was all but extinguished during the Soviet times. Today, perhaps the greatest challenge is to live as a "remnant community" in societies that are predominately secular and even hostile to religion. Estonia, for example, has a smaller percentage of people who confess any faith than any other country, except the Czech Republic. For that very reason, we specifically invited Bishop Alsted to contribute to this book. What does it mean to witness in a world where the Church is a minority community in a culture and society which does not readily reinforce the Church's values and life? And where do we find hope in that context?

ENTREPRENEURS DO NOT remain paralyzed by fear: they act. Entrepreneurs seize opportunities and do not worry about making mistakes. Like Paul, who vastly expanded the Gospel message by the power of the Holy Spirit[6], these go-getters are not afraid to enter the doors God opens for them.

Artur is one of these entrepreneurs. He serves in a town called Jõhvi, in the northern part of Estonia close to the Russian border. This town has become a ministry center for the area's United Methodist Church. Several pastors have been raised in this dynamic Estonian- and Russian-speaking congregation. Artur also serves as the director of Camp Gideon, which is located just outside of Jõhvi.

God has given Artur a bold vision. Artur has identified needs in his community and has empowered strong leaders to help him take steps to fill these needs. One of the most recent steps is the opening of Sunbeam, a day center for children with disabilities. The center offers care for the physical, developmental and spiritual needs of approximately 100 children. It is the only place of its kind in northeast Estonia. The long-term vision is to add a school program to the center.

Entrepreneurs can find opportunities for mission all around them. The migration of Russians into neighboring Finland was one such opportunity. When Pastor Artur learned that several of his church members were moving to study or work in the Finnish capital of Helsinki, he wondered if there might be a need for a Russian-speaking faith community in the city—and there was. Today, the Jõhvi preaching point in Helsinki is well on its way to becoming a church plant. It has many mission-minded leaders who are aiming to reach Russian-speaking youth and young adults in the Helsinki area of Finland. They have a vision of creating Russian-speaking United Methodist churches in all major cities in Finland.

What is happening in Jõhvi is just one example of what God has been doing in Northern Europe. This ministry is surprising and creative—this is what the Church must be in its new

6 Acts 16:6ff

future. When we see needs and opportunities in our communities, we must not be afraid to be bold.

Living in unknown territory

Some years ago, I was serving as pastor in a church with an extensive music ministry. On a weekly basis, approximately 150 people would be singing in the church's four gospel choirs.[7]

The most exciting part of this ministry was that the majority of the singers were non-Christians! I made it a priority to sing with the choirs and build relationships. Every week I would do a devotional and pray in one or two of the choirs. They made a challenging and exciting congregation. The best time, however, was after rehearsal was over when a dozen or so of us would go to a café to have coffee or a beer and talk. That was when we would have good existential conversations and quite often the conversation would revolve around Christian life: What is faith? How do you pray? Who is Jesus? How do you experience God? Why does God allow suffering? Most of these people did not have a Church background, but they were deeply interested in discussing these questions.

One of the tenors in the choir was a partner in a coaching company. He invited me to be part of the advisory board, whose purpose was to put pressure on the coaches and challenge them to think about difficult questions like: What defines us as human beings? What does it mean to make a choice?

One evening, after a choir rehearsal, my friend said: "Sometimes in the middle of a coaching session I can be filled with a deep love for my coachee and a deep desire to help him or her to a better life. What is happening to me?"

I responded, "I think that God may be moving in your life… "

He nodded thoughtfully.

---

7 African American gospel music inspired by people like Kirk Franklin, Fred Hammond, John P. Kee a.o.

Changing context

As a Church, what context are we facing? Let me tell you—I have absolutely no clue. There have been many changes in the Nordic countries over the past 40 years. We have moved from being a relatively homogeneous culture to becoming increasingly complex and highly diverse since the 1970s. Meanwhile, in the Baltic countries, this development began in the mid-'90s with the fall of the Soviet Union and a new spirit of independence emerged in these formerly oppressed nations. In these places, cultural change happened very quickly. Instead of being controlled by Russia, these countries have been rapidly influenced by the values and culture of the Western world.

Some people might label the Nordic and Baltic culture postmodern, but that would be far too simplistic. There are many cultures and subcultures that make up these nations. Postmodern is one of many labels that we could give to these nations. Like in the United States and the rest of the Western world, people today are more skeptical and more willing to ask difficult questions about the status quo.

I believe but I am not religious

People are generally turning their backs on organized religion, particularly the institutional Church, and yet many still believe in something. The perception of God is usually homemade and quite personal. General Secretary of the Danish Bible-Society Morten Thomsen Højsgaard uses the term "Google-Buddhists"[8] to describe this western self-centered spirituality. He explains that there is really no God in Buddhism, and on Google you decide for yourself what you are looking for.

---

8 Den Tredje Reformation (The Third Reformation), Morten Thomsen Højsgaard

For most Northern Europeans, faith is for special occasions. When a crisis occurs, faith becomes a model to explain or to cope with reality in an acceptable way. This may offer some sense of security for everyday life.

The Nordic and Baltic regions relate to the Church in different ways. Many people in the Nordic countries choose to do without organized religion, which comes with all its doctrines and boundaries. However, they typically return to the Church for transitional rites, like baptism and marriage.

In the Baltic countries, the situation is a little different. The Christian Church has not had the advantage of uninterrupted impact on the culture for centuries. As a result, the countries have a far weaker cultural tie to the Church. For example, according to a Eurobarometer poll in 2007, only 16 percent of people in Estonia said they believe in God. This puts Estonia (along with the Czech Republic) at the very top of the list of the most secular countries in Europe. On the other hand, as many as 70 percent of Estonians claim they believe in the existence of some sort of spirit or life force. They are spiritual, but not religious.

From dream to nightmare

In 1910, things were different. The churches in Europe embraced the perception that the Western culture was genuinely Christian. Their task was to evangelize the rest of the world. Mission societies, mission organizations and leaders gathered with their wealth of knowledge and experience in Edinburgh with the noble task to consider how to evangelize the world. We were at a high point of the modern Western missionary movement. But what no one knew was that the movement had in fact peaked and the strengths of the European mission societies were fading.

In the shadow of the miserable 1930s, T.S. Eliot wrote the book, *The Idea of a Christian Society*. Europe was drifting towards a new world war, millions were facing unemployment and the European governments were helplessly trying to deal with economic forces they could neither control nor understand. Eliot had seen young people rejecting the ideology of liberal capitalism and proclaiming a new ideology with the aim of freeing their nations from economic forces and leading them into a better future. Eliot, along with other Christian thinkers, asked: "If small, determined minorities can shape the future negatively using the powers of pagan ideologies like Communism and Fascism, what might a Christian minority be able to do to impart a whole nation with a positive sense of purpose directed by the Christian faith?"

In response to Eliot, Oxford economist D. L. Munby wrote the book, *The Idea of a Secular Society* in 1960. Munby advised Christians to reject Eliot's vision and to embrace the idea of a secular society. In his understanding, a secular society would not lead to marginalization of religion. Instead, a secular society would be governed by beliefs shared by all enlightened people, and there would be freedom for all to profess and practice their religious or nonreligious beliefs. Munby articulated the hope of peaceful coexistence between religions and other worldviews. Many people, among them many Christians, embraced the idea of a secular society. At the time, Munby's idea was an intriguing dream. Today, many pastors and Church leaders perceive it as a nightmare.

The evolution of the Church's mission

From the very beginning the Christian movement was characterized by local communities of faith called together in small groups, then sent out into the world. The Church was mission. The vision was clear and there was a high level of involvement.

When Emperor Constantine turned Christianity into the official religion of the Roman Empire[9], a new model called

9 In 318 AD Emperor Constantin with the Edict of Milan legalized Christian worship and became the patron of the church. In 380 AD

"Christendom" emerged. In Christendom, or Constantinian thinking, the congregation was the Church and the Church was the state. Mission was to those "outside of the empire" and closely related to the expansion of the empire either literally or more indirectly in securing the loyalty of states.

Mission had strong political implications in this era. When Christianity came to Norway and to Denmark (11th century), it was the kings who were baptized first. The royalty then decided that their nation would be Christian and everybody must be baptized. The desire of Christendom was to create uniformity—one church in one place should in all ways be like any other church in any other place. The life of the Church became generally unchangeable and all new things were initiated with the intention of becoming permanent.

Constantine's model of Church dominated for approximately 1,200 years. It was shaken when Martin Luther introduced the concept of the "priesthood of all believers." Luther preached that laypeople (not just the ordained!) had a ministry in the Church. If all Christians are pastors, the state starts to lose control of the Church. The priesthood of all believers was a potentially revolutionary idea.

However, the Church was too strong a force in society for the European states to give up on their control. While new churches had emerged and separated from the Catholic Church, these new Protestant churches soon were closely tied to the state as well. The priesthood of all believers remained an important theological thought that was never really accepted. Today, as then, it is still the ordained priesthood that preaches the Gospel, administers the sacraments and shapes the life in the churches.

In Luther's time, the Church had the perception of existing in a culture that was Christian and felt a responsibility to share

---

the Edict of Thessalonica, also known as *Cunctos populos*, was issued. It ordered all subjects of the Roman Empire to profess the faith of the bishops of Rome and Alexandria, making Nicene Christianity the state religion of the Roman Empire.

their faith. Mission took place outside of Europe and Christianity was spread all over the world—usually hand in hand with the export of European culture and values, which may not have been as "Christian" as the Europeans thought they were.

In Northern Europe we may think our problem is all about this state church or majority Church mindset. "If only the state church would repent and turn from its wicked ways and be released from its Constantinian captivity, things would immediately change for the better," I heard a visiting professor from Madagascar say in a seminar on mission a few years ago. But it may not be as simple as that. Some Constantinian thinking prevails, even in the Methodist Church. Our *Book of Worship*, the *Book of Discipline*, our hymnals, even our connectional thinking, which we are so proud of, may well have its origin in a Constantinian state church mindset.

Mission just outside the door

As early as the 1960s, signs of a coming paradigm shift started to appear. People began to make the shocking discovery that the world had changed. Now mission was no longer only in distant places like Africa or Asia—mission was needed right outside the door of our churches.

However, this cultural shift didn't affect the state churches much. They continued to rely heavily on the advantages of their relationship to the state. After all, Christianity was still taught in the schools, membership was still high, and while worship attendance was rapidly decreasing, the financial foundation was still solid. In independent free churches like the Methodist Church, we circled the wagons. We became much more occupied with life inside the church, caring for each other and protecting what was already there. The innovative times of starting new churches, developing social ministries, daring to try new things and daring to fail slowly disappeared.

Church leaders responded in a variety of ways. Some Christians responded by developing new programs adapted to the culture. Some studied Church growth from America. Some defended the moral positions of the Church and tried to hold on to what used to work. Others closed their eyes, said a silent prayer and hoped for the best. And some still live with the self-deception that our culture is Christian—the majority of children are still baptized, people still know the Church is there, and they do go to church at least at Christmas. To some people this is not bad at all.

Looking at the Nordic countries today, and even more so the Baltic countries, we are in a place that we have never been in before. We are in a mission situation. In some countries, as much as 85 percent of the population may still be members of a church. The challenge is not that the Methodists are a small minority under pressure from a majority Church; the challenge is that all Christians are a minority in a pagan environment. And we are only beginning to realize this.

Moving into this new territory

The Church in the Western world may be in the midst of one the most significant changes in its history, perhaps an even more substantial change than the Reformation. I am not talking about small cosmetic changes that can be addressed by a slight change in the worship service, by creating a rock and roll church, a Taizé devotional, a pilgrimage, a youth church or another niche enterprise. A paradigmatic shift is coming and it will involve a change at the core.

When paradigms change, roles and relationships between people change and new structures evolve. Old directions and values disappear and new ones emerge. There is confusion and turmoil. And we who live through this are in limbo. We have left the old paradigm, but the new one has not yet emerged.

What the new paradigm will involve is impossible to say yet, but there is little doubt that it will entail more change than is comfortable. There are still those who weep over the fact that our society and cultures have become so secularized that Christian values are abandoned and the Church has lost its influence. But the perception that the Church needs a kind of Christian culture that supports it and helps shape the new generations belongs to a Constantinian paradigm. We no longer live in a Constantinian world. The Church may never experience a time like that again.

The label frequently used to describe the current development is secularization. Missiologist Lesslie Newbigin suggests a different perception: "We have learned, I think, that what has come into being is a not a secular society, but a pagan society, not a society devoid of public images but a society which worships gods which are not God."[10]

This move toward a pagan society has taken several decades in the Nordic countries, but it seems the Baltic states managed to do it in less than two decades. In the Baltics, we gained freedom from communist secularism, became hungry for the Gospel and religion in the mid to late 1990s and by 2014 had transformed into the most secular and materialistic societies in the world.

Where is our hope?

With all these factors working against the Christian Church in Northern Europe, is there any hope for a brighter future?

Rather than mourning the loss of a Christian culture, we may perceive our current reality as a golden opportunity. It is a gift from God, to re-learn what it means to be a community of Christ-followers living among people without any Christian memory or understanding. To be Church in today's Northern Europe now means to be a people called by Jesus Christ to embody a social and spiritual alternative to the Nordic and Baltic culture. To be faithful to our Master, we must look our society straight in the eyes and make the culture accountable

10 *The Gospel in a Pluralist Society*, Lesslie Newbigin

to the Gospel—and thus we are back at the starting point—our original calling to be those small bands of disciples who confront their world and make disciples of Jesus Christ so that this the world may be transformed.

What you have is what you need

Listening to the teaching of a megachurch pastor who led his church from virtually nothing to 5,000 in worship and then visiting a 2,000-member church in the United States, a pastor may be tempted to join the "if only" game. We look at the big "made-in-the-USA" church with high attendance; a pastor in the ecclesial super-league; high quality, high impact ministries; and a top- tuned staff and well-equipped facilities. Everything seems to say, "this is church as it should be." Many Northern European pastors have listened to stories of rapid church growth and some have even made visits to these places. The *if only* game is on and it is a dangerous game to play, since it frequently overlooks reality and leads to apathy and disappointment. Meanwhile, the small made-in-Europe church, with 50 people in attendance, a pastor in the ecclesial minor league, a few average ministries, a group of hard-working volunteers and a less than adequate facility seems to hold little promise for a brighter future.

If only we had the resources. *If only* we had the staff. *If only* we were in a society where more than 20 percent of people attend worship every week. But we are not. We are in an environment where no more than 2 percent attend worship every week. And yet, I say to the Church, *that unless there is a mighty move by God in the Nordic and Baltic countries, The United Methodist Church will probably never be more than 5-10 times bigger than we are today.* However, I firmly believe that the small church is fully equipped to carry out God's mission in the world. We don't need more staff or better resources to make disciples—everything we need is already given by God.

The small church at its best has several things going for it. In the small congregation, you are seen and known. There is genuine interest and concern among people, and they often share stories and learn from each other. The church is often multi-generational, and the fellowship becomes a family. People try to live what they teach, and they are not afraid to share their shortcomings and failures.

When a small church is at its best, programs do not need to be run by employed staff. Church members are encouraged to discover their spiritual gifts and passions and to serve with those gifts inside and outside the church. There is high accountability to the values of the church, but very little micromanaging. The small church can make changes quickly; it can adjust to accommodate new mission opportunities without long and complicated decision processes. The focus of programs is to meet needs nobody else is meeting. In short, the small church is intimate, authentic, agile, involving and flexible.

The small church has the three main resources the Church has always relied on: people, the message of Jesus Christ and the strength of the Holy Spirit.

In less than 100 years, the Christian church spread to the whole area around the Mediterranean Sea, not relying on church buildings, sound equipment, keyboards, web pages, Facebook, Twitter, video projectors or any of the other stuff we believe we need to be Church. They didn't even have coffee! But those small clusters of disciples spread the Good News and ultimately changed the world.

The small church works

Some say it can't be done. These people need to get out of the way of those who are actually already doing it. In Norway, 15 local churches know this by experience. For several years they have made use of the Natural Church Development program, focusing on the quality of their life and ministry. They measure their strength in eight key areas: empowering leadership, gift-based ministry, passionate spirituality, effective structures, inspiring worship, holistic small groups, need-oriented evangelism and loving relationships. Then they work purposefully on strengthening their weakest areas. Leaders concentrate on empowering other Christians to serve, and they help them assess their gifts and graces to develop their God-given potential to the benefit of the whole body. These churches encourage people to live committed lives and to practice their faith with joy and enthusiasm. This is fueled through a personal devotional life and the participation in a small group. These small groups talk about the biblical texts and apply them to their daily lives, share personal concerns, pray for each other and learn to serve others both inside and outside the group.

These churches know that effective structures are essential to facilitate their development and they creatively organize to be able to pursue their primary task and mission in the context of their community.[11]

They persistently focus their evangelistic and diaconal efforts on the needs of the people around them and they are particularly attentive to the needs of non-Christians. (It all sounds like the Wesley Class Meeting and the early Wesleyan revival strategy, doesn't it?)

These are not large churches, but they are, by the grace of God, making use of the resources they have available. It is not surprising that they are becoming increasingly healthy and consistently receive new members.

In Odense, speaking of God's love

They want to be unambiguous when they speak of God's love in The United Methodist Church in Odense, Denmark. The Church has been in the process of changing over the past 10 years—from being a fairly traditional Church, with a good

---

11 BoD 2012, paragraph 243

outreach ministry among youth, to being a mission-driven Church focused on non-Christians, with the desire to help them become whole-hearted followers of Jesus Christ. Pastor Thomas emphasizes the team effort in this process, where the combination of seasoned and less experienced leaders with the right mix of gifts and a long-term commitment to the process has been essential.

Music, particularly African-American gospel music, has been the major door opener to hundreds of non-Christians coming to the church to sing, to listen and to be part of the community. The explicit message in the songs and the emotional power of the music is compelling. The music, in combination with a warm fellowship, good preaching and prayer, has made church out of the choir ministry, rather than making the choirs a ministry of the church.

The transformation of the congregation and the many new people in the church has put great challenges on the leadership. They have worked creatively to help people become part of the community, introduce them to Christ, lead them into discipleship and send them out to serve others. At the same time, they still work on keeping the doors as open as possible to reach even more people.

In Kokkola, prayer at the center

Towards the northeastern part of the Bay of Bothnia, we find the city of Kokkola. Ten years ago, the United Methodist presence was a church building and 2 elderly women. Today it is a thriving multicultural church with a vibrant ministry. The congregation outgrew the church some time ago, and now they worship in a school. The church has been turned into a coffeehouse, "Café Livingroom," with live music on weekends and a meeting place for groups in the congregation during the week. It all started with prayer and a vision to reach people in the city with a cross-cultural twist. In fact, before they even began, the pastor's husband bought headphones for translation because he believed they were going to need to worship in multiple languages.

Prayer continues to be the heartbeat of the congregation, and the weekly prayer meetings are a powerhouse in the life of the church, as are the many small groups meeting in homes. Under the leadership of Pastor Camilla, this church makes disciples and equips and empowers leaders to serve in the community and beyond.

I will let Camilla share what it means to be in ministry with people from across the world building the kingdom of Christ:

> *In a church with young people and families, inter-national and national students, there are many lessons to learn. One of them is to let people go. This happens all the time in my church. People come and go, not because they dislike us, but because they have to move to another country or another city. In the beginning this made me very frustrated. I've cried more than once when a person who became a vital part of the body suddenly moved away. It felt as if I was building a house of cards that continually fell apart. In my mind, I had a vision of a growing church. In practice, I had an airport where people landed for a while and then took off.*
>
> *In order to survive, I had to reshape my thinking. We are not building our little kingdom. We are to receive, train and send God's people away.*

Focusing on our mission

These stories show what can happen when small churches discover a clear sense of purpose and take advantage of the opportunities before them. When we peel off the layers of what we often understand as Church, we come to basically three relations: Up (to Christ), In (to other Christians) and Out (to our community). I usually illustrate this with a triangle.

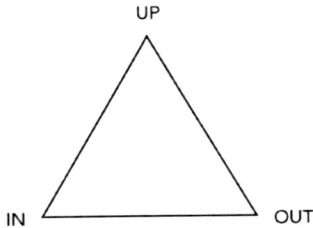

Up towards Christ. This is our personal and communal relationship with the living God, nurtured by worship and devotional life. This relationship is the starting point for anything we hope to accomplish.

In to other Christians. We are called to live and be in fellowship with other Christians—growing, learning, sharing and serving together.

Out to the community; towards the people and the world around us. Our primary task is to make disciples of Jesus Christ and through transformed people we believe the world will be transformed. This triangle describes the non-negotiables of what Church is.

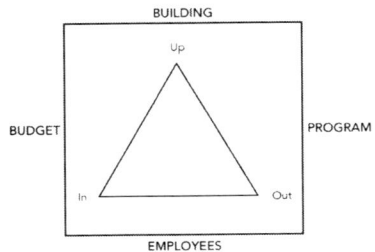

However, this triangle is often not enough for us. We often feel that to "really be Church" we must have additional elements. We need **employees**—first and foremost a pastor. Then we need a **building**, for worship and church life. With a church building we need **programs**, and finally we need a **budget** to pay for everything. These things are not bad, and in fact they are sometimes even necessary—however in all too many situations these elements overtake the majority of our time,

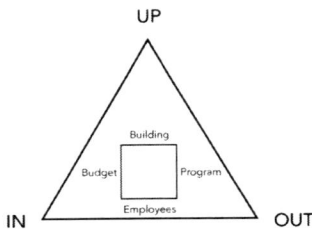

attention and resources, as illustrated by the rectangle surrounding the triangle.

Truthfully, employees, buildings, programming and budgets are all negotiable. A better way to look at the life and work of the church, regardless of its size, is to perceive these things as existing within the larger concern of the mission of the church. This creates a healthy balance between the primary relationships of the church and the functions of the church, as illustrated by the rectangle surrounded by triangle.

The church is an organism which grows in three dimensions, not just one. A church that is growing numerically is not necessarily healthy, while a healthy church will be growing in all three dimensions. The church will grow stronger in power and love through worship and discipleship (relation Up). It will grow warmer and deeper through fellowship and the use of the means of grace (relation In). And it will grow larger and broader through discipleship and ministry with the poor (relation Out).

Following Jesus into the world

After the resurrection, seven of the disciples gathered together. They had already met the risen Christ but still they were confused, insecure and perhaps even scared. What do you do when you don't know what to do? You make it simple and go back to where you started, doing the things you know how to do. Simon Peter said, *"I'm going fishing."*

And the others said: *"We'll go with you."* Then they went fishing, back to the Sea of Galilee where it all started.

They fish all night[12] and end up empty handed, no fish. But when a stranger on the seaside asks them to try again on the right side of the boat everything changes. The others, before Simon Peter, realize that the stranger must be the risen Jesus. Simon Peter jumps out of the boat, eager to get to the shore. This is when Simon Peter has a defining conversation with

---

12 Luke 5: 5

Jesus. Jesus is not addressing the confident believer, Peter, "the rock." He is taking Simon, son of John back to his primary calling. It all boils down to this one question, *"Simon, son of John do you love me?"* And then the two words: *"Follow me."*

Lesslie Newbigin describes what this means in a European pagan culture:

> *… We must be clear about what discipleship will mean. It cannot mean that one accepts the lordship of Christ, while sovereignty is acknowledged for the public life of society. It cannot mean that the Church is seen as a voluntary society of individuals who have decided to follow Jesus in their personal lives, a society which does not challenge the assumptions, which govern the worlds of politics, economics, education and culture.*
>
> *The model for all Christian discipleship is given once and for all in the ministry of Jesus. His ministry entailed the calling of individual men and women to personal costly discipleship, but at the same time it challenged the principalities and powers, the ruler of this world, and the cross was the price paid for that challenge. I do not think any of us knows what this will involve.*
>
> *We have accepted for too long the position of a voluntary society among other such societies, conceived as alternative options within a religiously and ideologically neutral society.*[13]

We are moving into new territory as a Church. As we seek to be faithful to our mission, even as a minority community in a pagan world, we look to the same spirit which inspired the early Church, which was also set in an alien culture. They transformed the world through the power of Jesus Christ. May

---

13 *The Gospel in a pluralist society, Lesslie Newbigin*

it be so for us in Northern Europe, in the U.S. and around the world.

—Bishop Christian Alsted

Bishop Christian Alsted was elected to the episcopacy in 2009. He oversees seven Annual Conferences in the Baltic and Nordic region of the Church. A native of Denmark, he was ordained in 1984 and received a Doctor of Ministry degree from Asbury Theological Seminary in 2012.

CHAPTER 5

The Death and Resurrection of the Church

A note from the editor: In preparing for this book, we intentionally chose two bishops who represent two very different contexts and experiences. The previous chapter by Bishop Christian Alsted offers a voice of hope for the Church, which finds itself as a minority in a thoroughly modern, materialistic and secular culture as represented by Northern Europe. In that context, the Church seeks to live out its witness in the face of decline and through the work of "small churches." Bishop John Innis writes from the context of the most rapidly growing branch of the Church, the Church in Africa. On the African continent, the Church faces incredible challenges of an entirely different sort including poverty, hunger, civil strife and suffering. And here, the Church is rapidly growing. Bishop Innis uses the metaphor of death and resurrection to discuss the life of the African Church and its continued growth.

THE DEATH AND resurrection of Christ is pivotal to the life and growth of the Church, especially in Africa. The central affirmation of the Church around the world is that Jesus Christ, who is the Bridegroom of the Church, died and rose again. So, the Church must die and be resurrected, for there is no resurrection without death. In dying the Church receives life, a new life and an abundant one. This is why the Church is called the "Easter people."

The Church in Africa

The Church in Africa has seen an exponential growth. This phenomenal growth is worth celebrating, and is occurring across mainline denominations, independent churches and Pentecostal-charismatic churches. Indeed, these churches have seen many conversions in Africa, and they continue to gain converts. The African Church has experienced rapid growth in many areas such as the number of baptisms, confirmations and ordinations that are occurring among them.

There has been a shift in global Christian populations. This shift can be seen in Sub-Saharan Africa, which has experienced one of the largest gains in Christian populations. For instance, during the 1900s, 90 percent of the Christian population was located in the Western world while only 10 percent was in Africa and two other parts of the world, namely Asia and Latin America. Today, about 68 percent of the Church exists outside the Western world, with the African Church having the largest portion of this percentage. The African Church is adding between 22,000 and 24,000 new believers every day.[14]

This remarkable growth of the African Church can be attributed to the work and ministry of indigenous Christians as well as international missionary work. The stunning expansion of the Church in Africa is affirmed in the words of one

14 Tennent, Timothy C., ed. "Interview with the President." The Asbury Herald. Vol. 123, no.1 (Spring 2013): 3

of Africa's leading theologians and writers, Dr. Lamin Sanneh. Sanneh states, "Africa has become, or is becoming, a Christian continent in cultural as well as numerical terms, while on the small scale the West has become, or is rapidly becoming, a post-Christian society."[15]

The Church must die

However, amidst growing numbers, the African Church is faced with daunting challenges. The widespread prosperity gospel and syncretistic Christianity (blending Christianity with existing traditions to the detriment of the Gospel) are just a few of our challenges. Although it can be safely said that in the mind of the African, there is no such thing as the "death" of the Church, the Church must die to these particular ideologies in order to be resurrected to new life.

As Church leaders, we can say that the Church is dying to "widespread prosperity theology," the money-focused message that focuses on success and materialism. In addition to teaching bad theology, the "prosperity gospel" exploits God's people financially. Also, the Church must die to "syncretistic practices," in which church members hold allegiance to African traditional practices that are not compatible to the Christian faith.

As the Church dies to these practices, the Church is being resurrected by her Savior and Lord. The resurrection of the Church in Africa can be seen in her growth, love and service. Indeed, the African Church has become a light and life to her people. The Church is growing at an unprecedented rate. New faith communities are being established across the continent and are impacting the lives of communities in a positive way.

---

15 Linder, Alex, ed. "The End of Western Christianity." Vanguard News Network Forum. July 12, 2008< http://www.vanguardnewsnetwork.com>

The African way of death

Part of what accounts for the growth of the Church is the way Africans understand death itself. In his book titled *African Religions and Philosophy*, John S. Mbiti writes: "Death is a separation but not annihilation because at the moment of death, the dead person becomes a living-dead." The concept of the "living-dead" in the African perspective means that when one dies, his or her spirit remains a part of the corporate life of the community. The dead remain a part of the spirit world, but communicate with the living through certain rituals.

Africans have a similar attitude about the Church. They do not feel the need to be physically present at all times. His or her presence may not always be visible, but the heart and mind of the Christian will stay connected to the community in many other ways. In this way, when an African becomes a Christian, his or her spirit becomes tied to the Church.

What we learn here from Mbiti is that Africans see the Church as the center of their lives. Everything else in life revolves around it. In the concept of the living-dead, the dead never depart from the living. The dead remain a part of the community through the spiritual realm. This is why in the African's mind the Church never dies—meaning the Church always remains a vital life-changing community of faith where people go to find meaning for their lives. When there is bad harvest during a farming season, for example, the church gathers to pray for good harvest; at the end of the prayer, farmers in the church would give testimony about God's goodness for good yield at the end of the farming season.

The African way to resurrection

The way the business of the Church is conducted in Africa is deeply rooted in the tradition of the African people. In Africa, no person is an island. The problem a single member faces in society becomes the collective concern of all other members. This mindset is the driving force that attracts people to the Church, and once they join the church community, they never want to turn back.

Families do some of the best evangelism for the Church in Africa. There is always a very strong family tie that binds members of the family together. When a family member who once practiced traditional religion goes to join a church, he or she goes out and tells others in the family about the connectedness and hospitality from the church.

The church in Africa seems to model herself after the early Church. We read in Acts:

> *They [the early church] devoted themselves to the apostles' teaching and to the fellowship, to sharing bread and to prayer. Everyone was filled with awe, and many wonders and signs were done by the apostles. All believers were together and had everything in common. Selling their possession and goods, they gave to one another as each had need. They broke bread and ate together in their homes and the Lord added to their number daily those who were being saved.*
>
> —*Acts 2:42-47*

This is the secret of the vitality and growth of the African Church. When people feel connected, and they feel a deep sense of love and hospitality, that is where they want to be.

Keys to resurrection and growth in the African Church

There are several common elements to the resurrection and growth of the Church in Africa:

- Most churches in Africa preach practical messages of salvation to win souls and not necessarily to attract more people to the Church. The essence of the Gospel proclamation is to make disciples. Good preaching, great music ministry and exciting worship experience may attract people to the Church, but it is love and genuine Christian hospitality that keep them there. The African Church takes these elements seriously and thus enhances the exponential growth of the Church.

- Authentic Christian service is a result of intentional biblical grounding, which is achieved through teaching in a practical way that is understandable to the people.
- African churches are experiencing rapid growth because they take teaching seriously. The Church in Africa is growing because Africans are intentional about discipleship and church growth.
- Authentic growth begins with a willing heart to serve God. Our first priority is to be obedient to the call of God. All other things will then fall in line. When we surrender to the will of God for our life and ministry, and allow God's purpose to reign over and against our will and desires, that's when success truly begins to happen. We ought to focus on the mission of the Church and discern God's will upon our lives to enhance that mission. In other words, as the Church, we are the ones called to take on the mission of God with a passion to make God's kingdom on earth a reality.

I had a friend in seminary who told me he was contemplating enrolling at a university to pursue a master's degree in administration and management. When I asked why, he told me he wanted to acquire skills in administration and management at the graduate level, which he strongly believes will help him solve problems he would face in the local church when he is appointed. My friend seemed to suggest that these classes would increase his chance of "success" in the local church. At this point, I knew my friend was misguided: University classes may offer education, but they will not guarantee success in making disciples or growing in faith. Obedience to the call of God must be the first priority for the resurrection of the Church.

Churches that grow are churches that center their life around the Lordship of Jesus Christ. The Church ought to reflect the love of Christ in all it does in the world. It must be different from the world and culture around it. The apostle Paul cautions: *"Therefore, if anyone is in Christ, he is a new creation; the old has gone, the new has come"* (2 Corinthians 5:17). When an African accepts Jesus as Lord and Savior, his or her life is modeled after Jesus. This new life in Christ is reflected in how the corporate church lives out its nature and mission in the world.

The vibrant growth of the Church in Africa is due to the African's resilient spirit and faith in her Lord and Savior, the Resurrected Christ. This faith is deeply anchored in the love of Christ and the belief that even death, in all its forms, will have no victory over the Church of Africa. Like Paul says in Romans 8:35-39:

> *Who will separate us from the love of Christ? Will hardship, or distress, or persecution, or famine, or nakedness, or peril, or sword? ... No, in all these things we are more than conquerors through him who loved us. For I am convinced that neither death nor life, nor angels, nor rulers, nor things present, nor things to come, nor powers, nor height, nor depth, nor anything else in all creation, will be able to separate us from the love of God in Christ Jesus our Lord.*

Paul's words represent the African Church's faith. The people of Africa are diverse and face many different problems. Many Africans face daily the devastation of civil wars, oppression, famine, poverty, demons and the onslaught of diseases like AIDS. And yet these problems are no longer insurmountable in the face of our faith. The Church in Africa shall remain alive because of her love for Christ!

Indeed, the Church in Africa can boast in the Lord for a new life and vibrancy, because of her death and resurrection. This is her hope and joy!

—*Bishop John Innis*

Bishop John Innis is assigned to the Liberia Area of The United Methodist Church. Prior to his election, he served as teacher, principal and pastor in Liberia. He is the former president of the Liberian Council of Churches and chairs the Commission on Central Conference Theological Education.

CHAPTER 6

Ebola: Hope in a Time of Hopelessness

A note from the editor: Bishop Innis submitted the preceding chapter several months before the outbreak of Ebola in his country. Given the urgency of this crisis, we invited Bishop Innis to offer his reflections on how the Church lives out its witness in the light of this overwhelming tragedy. Immediately, the question moved from the theology of the death and resurrection of the Church to the Church's witness in a time of hopelessness and death. Bishop Innis graciously agreed to share his thoughts as we join with United Methodists around the world in a prayer of hope for Liberia and all of Western Africa.

LIKE DEATH, WHICH brings hopelessness and despair to people everywhere, the resurrection of Jesus Christ brings hope and courage to all who put their trust in Him. The Church in West Africa holds to this truth despite the fear, misunderstanding, hopelessness and physical pain that is being experienced by the people there as a result of the Ebola epidemic. This virus has caused agony, heartbreaking loss and catastrophe in Liberia, Sierra Leone and Guinea.

The impact of the Ebola epidemic

The Ebola virus disease, according to health practitioners, is a severe, often fatal, illness for humans. This virus is transmitted to people from animals such as the large fruit bat, monkeys and baboons.[16]

Similarly, it is spread in the human population through human-to-human transmission. Signs and symptoms of this virus are fever, strong headache, muscle soreness or pain, weakness or loss of appetite, diarrhea, vomiting, abdominal pain and unexplained rashes, bruising, blistering or bleeding. The signs and symptoms usually start between two days and three weeks after contracting the virus. Previous outbreaks of this virus have happened in the Sudan, Gabon, Uganda, Zaire/Congo and D.R. Congo, to name a few. Recently, Liberia, Sierra Leone, and Guinea have been attacked by the virus. This is unprecedented.

Liberia, still suffering from the emotional wounds of 14 years of civil war and the struggle to overcome poverty, was hard hit by the deadliest and most massive Ebola outbreak in history. This horrible and deadly virus has killed dozens of healthcare workers and swept away entire households in the twinkling of an eye, leaving us with orphans. Also, this virus attacked our fragile health system, leaving it completely overstretched. We witnessed the deaths of our people from treatable diseases because they could not get into hospitals. These people became sick as a consequence of the virus. Likewise, the Ebola treatment units (ETU) built to hold Ebola patients were full and became so overwhelmed that they were constrained to refuse new Ebola patients. Thus, we watched some of our people die at hospital gates and witnessed corpses lying in our streets for days.

Further, in an effort to contain the spread of this fatal virus, the government of Liberia put in place the following measures:

16 Nisbett, Richard A. Ebola Disease Facts. Monrovia, Liberia: Discipleship Resources International, 2014.

announced a state of emergency and curfew; ordered a stay-at-home for all nonessential government employees (public and private institutions applied this measure to their employees); ordered the closure of all schools in the country for an indefinite amount of time; and quarantined epicenters, among other safeguards. Furthermore, the epidemic created economic and untold hardship for the Liberian populace. The price of food escalated, wages of some institutions were not paid and businesses were wrecked. In addition, Liberians have been stigmatized, excluded and abandoned by some foreign countries because of the health crisis.

Consequently, we stood and looked sadly at the massive exodus of some of our Liberian sisters and brothers as well as some members of the international community for fear of the Ebola virus. Our country has become virtually paralyzed. In the midst of the grim reality of the Ebola catastrophe that has ravaged our land and killed our dear compatriots, our people may wonder whether there is hope. The deadly pandemic has created a situation of death and hopelessness. The virus has bred pessimism and despair.

Light at the end of the tunnel

In light of the Ebola virus disease that is plaguing our land and thrown us back so badly, questions arise: Is there any hope? With gloom looming over us as a nation and people, will we resurrect from this uncertainty? How can the people of Liberia and West Africa experience hope in the time of hopelessness? Where is God in all of this? Is God going to rescue us? How can we explain God's love in the furnace of pain or the web of fear or a state of uncertainty? Are the hands of the Lord with us?

The answer is: *Yes! There is hope. There is no situation that is beyond the intervention and redemption of God.*

From the Old Testament, we find in Ezekiel 37:1-14 the vision of the valley of dry bones. In this vision, we see a situation of utter and complete hopelessness in which the Israelites found themselves. The prophet Ezekiel is driven by the Spirit to a valley full of lifeless bones, and there he is engaged in a dueling conversation by God. God wishes to transform this valley of death into a valley of life and hope. In Ezekiel's vision, the dry bones were resurrected—a symbol of Israel's restoration. The lesson from this vision is that God can change situations that appear totally hopeless—even ones like the Ebola pandemic that has created the situation of death and hopelessness. God can transform the very space of death and hopelessness to hope. Therefore, it is incumbent upon all of God's children to never give up but put their hope in the Lord, even in the face of apparent insurmountable obstacles.

As Christians, the Bible tells us that our lives are held within the love of God in Christ Jesus. In Romans 8:31-39, we see God's plan for his people, which reveals that we live from the promise that nothing can ever separate us from the love of God. This does not mean if bad things happen to us that God no longer loves us. God loves us even when we live in a world of uncertainty, frustration, tragedy and despair. Instead, it means disease (Ebola), hardship, trouble, disaster, hunger, feelings, and even death cannot break God's solidarity with us.[17]

Moreover, we know from Scripture that the promises of God are sure. When the situation appears bleak from a human perspective and we are overwhelmed by the situation, our most likely response is to become confused or angry, which only compounds our suffering. We go through this unnecessary experience because we fail to trust in the promises of God. We need to learn to trust in the promises God has given to us as his people through faith in Christ.

---

17 World Council of Churches. Facing Aids The Challenge, the Churches' Response. Geneva: WCC Publication, 2002.

Living in hope because God is with us

God's people are called to live by hope in Jesus Christ only. It is Christ who is with us in our suffering and struggle as He carries us through. And it is in Christ alone that Christians can see beyond the smell of hopelessness to the unspeakable joy that hope brings. Through the Holy Spirit, we experience God's promise to be with us in our distress—comforting us, never to leave us alone nor forsake us.

In this Ebola crisis, the Lord has been with the people of Liberia, Sierra Leone and Guinea. Through His mercy and faithfulness, we are experiencing a downward trend in the spread of Ebola. There is a drop in the number of Ebola cases; Ebola treatment units are becoming empty as many survivors walk out; there is massive support from the international community for our affected countries in the fight against the virus; and our people are whole-heartedly involved in the fight. In the midst of all this, the African Church is optimistic to eradicate Ebola from our lands as the Church seeks to make more disciples for Christ. To use the words of John Wesley, the best we can say is that "God is with us."

—Bishop John Innis

CHAPTER 7

New Life in the Third Place

AT A MACRO level, the statistics are clear and sobering: The mainline Church in the United States has been in decline, by every conceivable measure, for more than a generation. This is truer in some geographical areas than others, and is more pronounced in some particular traditions than in others. Within this trend The United Methodist Church has not been an outlier. We have participated and contributed to the fragility of the Church in American culture. And yet, for those with eyes to see and ears to hear, there are exceptions. As Paul Tillich the noted theologian of the last century wrote: "Here and there, now and then, there is a new creation."

The new creation

The new creation is always a gift of God's grace—a movement of the Holy Spirit. And sometimes we come across such a discovery when we had almost ceased looking. For a time, I served as a district superintendent in the mountains of western North Carolina. The small United Methodist Church in Bryson City had been in decline for a generation. It was sustained by faithful men and women who knew the hymns, recited the creeds, read the daily Upper Room and contributed to the local church and beyond—yet the average age of the membership was creeping steadily upward.

The retirement of a dedicated pastor led to the assignment of a younger pastor, who happened to have an affinity with the mountains in general and canoeing and kayaking in particular. This pastor, Wayne Dickert, was assigned to the Bryson City Church. He had the additional mandate to begin a worshipping community at the nearby Nantahala Outdoor Center. Wayne (nicknamed "Wayner" by a coach along the way) was a legend in the canoeing and kayaking community and had built a high level of trust with the Outdoor Center. He began a conversation, which led to a community. This led, in time, to a seasonal service from May through September of each year.

And so, on a typical Sunday morning during the late spring, summer and early fall, the service on the Nantahala River, which is known as the "River of Life," gathers a community for singing, prayer, Scripture reading and reflection. One of the movements of the service is an invitation to walk the short distance down to the river, where one touches the water; when I experienced this moment, I was reminded of my baptism. As the community matured it began to look outward, and the congregation began to raise funds to dig wells in Haiti. This was an amazingly organic and fitting missional engagement with brothers and sisters in need of life-giving water!

Later on each Sunday morning, there is worship in the sanctuary of the church. In the off-season, some of the River of Life participants find their way to the church, but this is not an expectation. Over time, with patience and integrity, Wayne has helped the River of Life community and the Bryson City UMC to see themselves as different and complementary expressions of the one Body of Christ.

If you were to attend both services on a given morning, you would meet a diverse group of people. At the River of Life, you might meet one or two retired persons, a few more approaching retirement, a healthy number of middle-aged adults, a larger number of young adults, an even larger number of youth and a healthy contingent of children. Later, in the sanctuary service, you would encounter an infant or two, two or three children, three or four young ones, a young adult here and there, a few middle-aged couples, a larger number of folks approaching retirement, an even larger number of retired members and a healthy contingent of mature and aging adults.

In reflecting on my experience at Bryson City, I have been struck that the people have discovered a model that would be helpful for our church, particularly in the United States. These two congregations are a mirror image of each other, and together they represent the larger community. Therein lies our hope. Here and there, now and then, there is new creation.

Discovering the "third place"

How did this sign of renewal come to be? Sociologists speak of the third place. The third place provides a hub for the community and a place for social interactions beyond the first two places—home and the workplace. In a Church culture, the third place was the church, and as a result the church was often the center of the community. But in a post-Christian culture, third places are varied: a coffee shop, a sports team, an online community. In the community adjacent to Bryson, the powerful and prominent third place is the Nantahala Outdoor Center. Enthusiasts come from long distances to enjoy the rapids; staff pursue their vocations as guides on the river; and businesses flourish around the core activities of rafting and canoeing.

Intuitively, the River of Life experiment is analogous to the recent development of "Fresh Expressions" in Great Britain, a movement begun by the Church of England and quickly adopted by the British Methodist Church. The method of Fresh Expressions is simple: to equip pioneering ministers (lay and clergy) to create fresh expressions for Christians in the culture. These will not replace traditional worship services, but exist alongside them. The term for this reality is called a "mixed economy" of church. The two worship services in Bryson, at 8:30 (on the river) and 10:55 (in the sanctuary) differ in style, location, target audience and missional focus. Yet, it is clear that they have a common purpose: to lead participants into an experience of God.

The beauty of the River of Life service is that it does not require a person to cross the threshold of a church building in order to worship God. Instead, it provides access to the worship of God in the midst of God's creation. In this way, it is indeed a "thin place"—to borrow a phrase from the Celtic Christian tradition that has also shaped the Smoky Mountains.

If our beloved United Methodist Church has "a future with hope"—and my prayer is that it does—it will surely replicate the experience of Bryson City and the River of Life. We will discover the emerging third places in our communities; we will call and equip the respected persons in those contexts to shape new forms of worship; we will attempt experiments large and small in the unlikeliest of places; and we will trust that the God who calls the Church into being desires her renewal and is endlessly creative and generative.

This discovery will be the spiritual practice of visionary leaders who discover the third place and claim the good news: "Here and there, now and then, there is a new creation."

—*Bishop Kenneth Carter*

Bishop Kenneth Carter is bishop of the Florida Area of The United Methodist Church. His relationship to the Bryson City United Methodist Church and their pastor, Wayne Dickert, was formed during his service as superintendent in the Western North Carolina Conference. He is a native of Georgia and graduate of Columbus College, Duke Divinity School, the University of Virginia and Princeton Theological Seminary. He has received honorary degrees from Bethune-Cookman University and the United Methodist University in Liberia.

CHAPTER 8

The Main Thing is to Keep the Main Thing the Main Thing

I AM ASHAMED to say that I cannot find my nose ring. Members of my Annual Conference and those who peruse my website may be surprised at my shame, because no one has ever seen me wearing a nose ring. Few people know that I own one. But I do. And I cannot find it.

The day of my consecration as a bishop of The United Methodist Church, my brother Greg and his wife, Susan, kindly gifted me with an assortment of rings as a gag gift. They joked that a bishop ought to have rings for people to kiss and a nose ring would supplement nicely the episcopal pin in my lapel. We all had a good laugh, and then went home. Mary Lou and I packed up the household and moved to Wichita, Kansas. After a brief sojourn in Topeka, the house was ready for us and we unpacked in late November. Somewhere in the moving process, my set of rings was put away in a box that, 10 years later, has not yet been opened and unpacked. I am sure it is in our basement somewhere, but I haven't seen it since 2004. My deep fear is that when I am reassigned to a new episcopal area, we will move that unopened box to our new home. Meanwhile, my brother keeps reminding me of my ingratitude for not wearing his gift of a nose ring.

The real point to this story is that I have some physical baggage in my basement that ought to be sorted and either used or discarded. (Whether there is a use for the nose ring remains to be seen. I have to find it first.) But I suspect I am not alone in having accumulated more things than I need and being weighed down by excess stuff. I am no longer nimble because I am hanging on to a lifetime of accumulated baggage. For me to move easily and well into my future will require cleaning the basement, sorting the possessions and deciding what is still useful. I am going to keep the scuba diving equipment that is down there so I am ready for my next trip to the beach. But my bank statements from the 1980s are probably ready for the recycle bin. It is time to leave them behind. Then there are the VHS tapes. Will I ever again watch a commercially produced movie in that format? Or does that box have some family videos I shot when the kids were little? I know that, with time and attention, I could sort this stuff and discard a lot. I should do that. It is time to be more nimble.

Resistance to change

Most of the local congregations and Annual Conferences of The United Methodist Church have accumulated a different kind of baggage. We have accumulated a variety of traditions and practices that can weigh us down. They form a kind of spiritual baggage that keeps us from easily moving to a new place and a new way of life. Because our faith and our church is a comfort to us, Christians naturally resist change. We want to keep serving God in the ways that we know and have come to cherish. But what if those ways are not working for our congregation? How do we know what is working and what is not? Most of us resist change, but sooner or later most of us must come to terms with the spiritual "stuff" we have been hanging on to. Eventually, it is time to clean out the basement.

Such a cleaning project will uncover many usable and underutilized things from the past. While my nose ring is not underutilized, I expect to find some pictures of my family that will be useful for the next family reunion. There is a suitcase down there I could be using in my travels. There are other treasures in the basement that I have forgotten about that I can use well in the future. These things come from my past, but they can be used to enrich my future. The cleaning-out process makes me distinguish between what is junk to be discarded and what is usable and should be brought upstairs into the new house.

New creation on the Great Plains

In January 2014, the Kansas East, Kansas West and Nebraska Annual Conferences came together to create the Great Plains Annual Conference. We made this decision to strengthen and reinvigorate the United Methodist mission in our two states. This story begins with an event that was not of our choosing: The number of bishops for the South Central Jurisdiction was reduced, meaning our states would share a single bishop as of September 1, 2012. Fortunately, the College of Bishops announced this change three years before it went into effect, which gave us time to plan for the future. A Transition Team started meeting in November 2009. The leadership of this 22-person team, along with the participation of both bishops and the consultation of the Rev. Gil Rendle, was crucial as we prepared for such a major change. Our team spent time studying the two states and focusing on our mission together on behalf of The United Methodist Church.

We knew that we needed to listen carefully to both clergy and laity in our Conferences as we prepared for the future. We invited them to think deeply about the issues involved in this change. We never doubted our United Methodist mission: "to make disciples of Jesus Christ for the transformation of the world." We were also committed to the second sentence of our denomination's mission statement, "Local churches provide the most significant arena through which disciple-making occurs." But we wanted to make our collective ministry as strong and missionally effective as possible, so we needed to think about our spiritual baggage. What are we doing well and what should we strengthen? What should we quit doing?

At the 2010 sessions of the three Conferences, we asked the people to consider three questions:

1. What is the missional purpose of the Annual Conferences?

2. How do we best develop lay and clergy leaders for these three Conferences?

3. Considering answers to the previous questions, is our mission best accomplished by three Conferences, two Conferences or one Conference?

A new beginning

After a great deal of conversation in all three Conferences, we presented a proposal for becoming one Conference to each of the three sessions in 2011. The team explained the reasons they thought becoming one Conference was the right step, and we took a "five-finger" vote allowing people to express a range of support or opposition. In this kind of vote, a show of five fingers represents strong support, 3 fingers means a voter has significant questions and 1 finger signifies strong opposition. At every step the team invited suggestions and questions from people in the Conferences.

In May and June of 2012 the three Conferences voted to become one Conference effective January 1, 2014. The proposal we voted on included key principles for the future, but not all the details were worked out. An affirmative vote meant that the three Conferences wanted to design something new, which would mean "cleaning out the basement." We would carry forward the best of the Conferences and leave behind some things that we no longer needed. The votes were sealed after the first Conference sessions. At the close of the Nebraska and Kansas East Conference sessions, Bishop Sherer-Simpson and I simultaneously announced overwhelming approval from all three groups.

The Transition Team stayed in place for another 15 months until a Uniting Conference could be held to approve a detailed Plan of Organization. In August 2013, all three groups met in the same room for a 48-hour conference. After thorough discussion, each Conference separately approved a 155-page plan that addressed important details for our new Conference, such as pensions, health insurance, Conference committees and structure and the budget.

Mission, calling and vision

I believe that the most important parts of the document were those that cast a vision for the future. A section labeled "Mission, Calling and Vision" says: "The mission of The United Methodist Church is to make disciples of Jesus Christ for the transformation of the world. The calling of the Great Plains United Methodist Conference is to equip and connect congregations to make disciples of Jesus Christ. The vision for the Great Plains—our preferred future—is captured in this phrase: Great churches. Great leaders. Great disciples. Transformed world."

We named four priorities:

1. Enhancing the ministry of local churches with Christ-centered excellence in: youth ministry, preaching and worship, engaging the community and transforming service to the world.

2. New church starts.

3. Leadership development for both clergy and laity of the Conference.

4. Strengthening global mission partnerships with Nigeria, Haiti and Zimbabwe.

The closing paragraph of the plan was labeled "Service to Christ." It reads:

> *Once this plan of organization is approved, the real work continues. As one Conference, the United Methodist clergy and laity of Nebraska and Kansas hereby recommit ourselves to the mission of making disciples of Jesus Christ for the transformation of the world. We are becoming one Conference with the clear goal of becoming even more fruitful and effective in service to Christ than we have been in the past. We undertake this mission trusting in the grace of our Lord Jesus Christ and the ever-present power of the Holy Spirit.*

We were casting a vision of what God might do through us in the future. Our priorities show how God might lead us from our present reality to our preferred future.

Key lessons from the Great Plains

Four key lessons can be learned from our experience in creating the Great Plains Conference.

First, leave useless baggage behind. People in religious communities are institutionally conservative and prefer to maintain their practices unchanged through time. The holier a practice is, the more resistant people are to making changes. Consider the out-of-date words used in the *Lord's Prayer*: "hallowed," "thy" and "trespasses." The "Apostle's Creed" uses "quick" to mean living, not speedy. People no longer use these words in daily conversation, but we use them often in church.

This reluctance to changing something so small helps us to understand why congregations resist larger changes, like altering the sanctuary or changing worship times. Even at the Annual Conference level, certain traditions can become so important that change is seen as a bad idea. The most controversial topic at one of my Annual Conferences during the last decade was changing our meeting place from our university to a local church. The debate lasted for more than an hour.

It's difficult to leave behind useless baggage. Few leaders make a careful analysis of whether our practices and structure are actually the best way to pursue our mission. In our case, the creation of a new Annual Conference gave us the opportunity to evaluate many aspects of our structure, our staffing, our budget and our practices. We got to leave behind the things that were no longer useful. Yet, for each piece of useless baggage, there was a person ready to defend its usefulness and argue for maintaining it.

Discarding baggage requires a leadership team diverse enough to represent the whole conference and visionary enough to make the hard choices about what should be left behind. In a local church, a long-range planning committee or vision team can do this work. For us, it was a dedicated Transition Team that was given authority to make plans and proposals and then receive feedback. Frequently they said "no" to suggestions to maintain parts of the old conference structures that were no longer needed.

The second lesson we learned is to ask the right questions. Discarding baggage that someone thinks is valuable requires a good reason. A church or Conference that seeks greater vitality must ask these key questions and find wide consensus for their answers:

- What is our mission?
- What is our calling?
- What are our priorities?

The main problem affecting congregations, conferences and denominations is that they have lost clarity about their purpose. In my experience, thriving congregations are those that have a clearly stated mission and are disciplined in pursuing that mission. They also are clear about their calling—they know how that mission is best followed in their time and place. For our Conference, we asked: "What is the particular role of a Conference in Kansas and Nebraska in pursing the mission of The United Methodist Church?" We also asked questions about our priorities: "What aspects of that calling were most important for us to work on?" These questions helped us cast a vision for a new, shared future.

The third lesson is to stay focused and not get distracted. Along the way there will be many voices seeking to make their concerns the greatest priority. The main thing is to keep the main thing the main thing. This statement, usually attributed to Steven Covey, is a reminder that we must remain focused on our mission and calling. In our process, there were difficult conversations about clergy pensions, health insurance for retired clergy, the salaries of district superintendents and our funding of related mission agencies. The Transition Team paid attention to these and other questions, but they also worked hard at being focused on the more important issues like revitalizing local churches, starting new churches, and raising up a new generation of Christian leaders.

The fourth lesson we learned is to cast a vision. Successful change requires casting a vision so people can imagine a new future. What might God do through us in the years ahead? How might God lead us from our present reality to something new? Our answers to these questions can help people get excited about the future.

If vision-casting is accompanied by concrete proposals for change, people will have questions. They will have objections and doubts. Dialogue is essential, because it allows vision-casters to clarify the vision, connect the vision to the changes proposed, and respond to the concerns raised.

Despite our best preparations, however, there will be people who vote no and refuse to make the journey to the new way of doing Church. We want as many people to catch our vision as possible, but those who refuse to take part should be respectfully and graciously allowed to exit and find other ways of serving Christ.

Finding hope in the transition

It is sometimes said that the only person who likes change is a baby with a wet diaper. Actually, many of us welcome change if we are sufficiently uncomfortable. The problem is that we haven't noticed our discomfort. The decline of United Methodism has been so slow and gradual that leaders at all levels of the Church have accepted our decreasing numbers without much willingness to change. We need to be honest about our collective reality—we cannot continue as we have been. We must clean out our basements.

I believe God has a great future in store for The United Methodist Church. The transition from where we are to what God has in store means reconnecting with our Wesleyan heritage and re-appropriating some of our forgotten resources. It means leaders have to be more assertive and more collaborative. By God's grace the Kansas East, Kansas West and Nebraska Annual Conferences were able to clean out their collective basements and create something new. We left many things behind. We kept the best practices from each of the Conferences. We stayed focus on our priorities. We did not accomplish everything that we wanted, but we made a lot of progress toward becoming a stronger and more fruitful Conference. What we accomplished in the Great Plains Conference is possible in many other places, whether local churches, Conferences or a whole denomination. God is certainly at work in The United Methodist Church and transformation of the whole United Methodist movement is indeed possible.

—*Bishop Scott Jones*

Bishop Scott Jones currently serves as the bishop for the Great Plains Area of The United Methodist Church with offices in Topeka and Wichita, Kansas and Lincoln, Nebraska. He is a native of Nashville, Tennessee and a graduate of the University of Kansas and Perkins Theological Seminary. He holds a doctorate from Southern Methodist University. He previously served as a pastor in Texas and as the McCreless Associate Professor of Evangelism at Perkins School of Theology. He is the author of four books, most recently, The Wesleyan Way: A Faith That Matters, published in 2013.

CHAPTER 9

Sparks of Hope

THE YEAR: 1992. The place: Sarajevo. The Bosnian War was at its height, and the beautiful capital city of Sarajevo was under siege. Looking out his apartment window, a gifted young musician watched in horror as a mortar shell landed outside in the street, killing 22 of his neighbors and friends who were standing in line waiting for bread. In the midst of his grief, the young musician wanted to do something in response to this immense tragedy. So he did what he knew to do—he took his cello to the place where his friends were killed, placed a chair in the middle of the crater, and began to play. For 22 days straight he came to that same place and played, in his words, to "daily offer a musical prayer for peace."

For the next 18 months, that musician played in ruined buildings and cemeteries across the city of Sarajevo. He was not just offering a musical prayer for peace—he was becoming a courageous symbol of hope. Hope that one day, peace will conquer violence. Hope that one day, beauty will conquer ugliness. Hope that one day, music will be heard instead of gunfire.

A resurrection people

Merriam-Webster's dictionary defines hope this way: "To cherish a desire with anticipation." This book is about that kind of hope for the Church. It's about where we see signs of hope—sparks that can kindle a flame of excitement about our future.

We have all heard facts, statistics and stories of the challenges facing The United Methodist Church. And those challenges are real and need to be addressed if our beloved denomination is to not simply survive but instead thrive. There are plenty of books and articles and sermons and speeches given about the difficulties of turning around an organization as complex as The United Methodist Church. However, in the midst of such dire predictions, we must also remember that we are a "resurrection people." Our faith is built upon hope. So, in the midst of the difficult messages we hear all around us, we also need to be reminded that there are stories of hopefulness throughout this great Church. We need to hear these stories.

When I was asked to share where I find hope in the United Methodist Church, my mind went immediately to one place: the people. For me, the hope of the United Methodist Church lies not in new structures or new programs or new ways of organizing. The hope of the Church is in its people.

Sharing faith leads to hope

When I served in the local church, I must admit that I never really enjoyed the administrative part of ministry. I did it, but mostly because I had to do it. Over the years, my churches got larger, and my administrative responsibilities increased. I wouldn't say my overall satisfaction with ministry increased along with those administrative duties. I was getting the "work" done, but it wasn't soul-filling. That's when I realized I was doing less and less of the very thing that had drawn me to ministry in the first place. And it wasn't the office work; it wasn't working with staff; it wasn't organizing schedules and meetings—it was the people. It was their stories of faith that strengthened my own faith. It was their sharing of their life experiences that deepened my appreciation for who they were. It was hearing how they had overcome obstacles that helped me when I felt I was stumbling. It was the people who gave me hope for my ministry and the larger Church. That realization changed the way I worked.

Catching the vision

When I felt frustrated or weary at the administrative responsibilities of a large church, I would leave the office and return to the stories of faith found in the people I served. I would go to the nursing homes; I would visit in homes; I would listen to them and their stories of faith; and I would be encouraged. Their lives were a touchstone for me, and a way for me to remember why I was doing what I was doing. It is the people who are the backbone of the vitality of the local church. For some, their faith is quiet and behind the scenes, an "out of the spotlight" kind of faith; with others it is more public. But it is that strength of faith interwoven with daily life that gives me hope for the future of the Church. In fact, for me, a vital congregation is one whose people have caught the vision of what a life in Christ truly means.

A vital congregation is one whose people know how to live out their faith

- through continued faith development
- through outreach to those beyond their walls
- through participation in worship that reminds them of the connection to the Divine

- through every aspect of their lives.

A vital congregation is one whose people understand that faith and life are not separate, but are intimately interwoven into the very fabric of who they are and how they live. And now, even though I no longer serve a local congregation, I have continued to find these stories of faith and hope, and they continue to warm my heart and inspire hope within my own soul.

So, I would like to introduce you to some of these people of faith in the hope that their stories might offer sparks of hope that can rekindle our own faith and move us to become the people God intends.

Many gifts, one spirit

There was a strange couple standing by the cookie table in the back of the sanctuary. The husband looked as though he had just gotten out of bed, with his hair sticking out in many directions and his clothes wrinkled and stained. The wife was wearing what looked like a loose-fitting wedding gown from Goodwill. In a fairly well-to-do kind of church, this visiting couple certainly stood out. They were happily eating cookies and drinking the punch, and when worship began, they marched down the center aisle and sat down in the front pew. They were regular attenders after that, appearing at any event where food was served. They never missed a Sunday, and they were always eager to talk. Their apartment was within easy walking distance of the church and they were thrilled to have found us!

I'm not proud of the fact that I often tried to avoid them— they would take so much of my time, especially on Sunday mornings. They would stay until the last cookie was put away and would even follow us as we locked the church and started on our way home. However, one Sunday we announced that a family in town had lost everything to a fire and we were collecting items to help them rebuild. That afternoon, the doorbell rang at the parsonage, and when I answered it, there stood this couple with a paper bag in their hand. They said something like this: "We heard about the family that lost everything, and we want to give them this." They handed me the bag, and left.

When I opened the paper bag I found inside a small picture of the Last Supper. This couple had meager possessions, but they were still able to give. And as I sat in my beautiful home, surrounded by my many "things," I wept as I realized this couple had taught me a lesson of faith: a lesson so simple and yet so profound that even now—more than 20 years later—it still brings me to tears.

> *Now there are varieties of gifts, but the same Spirit; and there are varieties of services, but the same Lord; and there are varieties of activities, but it is the same God who activates all of them in everyone. To each is given the manifestation of the Spirit for the common good.*
>
> *—1 Corinthians 12:4-6*

I find hope in the belief that we all have something to offer. We all can learn from each other. In fact, it's more than that—we need each other—in all our diversity. Only then can we truly be the Body of Christ.

One small act

One winter day, a little girl in a small struggling rural church heard a presentation about a United Methodist ministry with Native Americans on a reservation up near the Canadian border. Well, this little girl heard the stories of children on the reservation who were unable to go to school because they had no coats. You see, without coats, the children weren't able to stand outside in the cold waiting for the school bus on those frigid winter mornings and therefore were unable to attend school. Now, this little girl probably heard some of the shocking statistics for that reservation—that it has a poverty rate of nearly 40 percent and a 75 percent rate of fetal alcohol syndrome. But mostly she was concerned because the children were cold. This little girl was so moved by the story that after church that Sunday, she took off her own coat and offered it to the pastor to give to the children there.

The reality is that one little coat cannot do much in the face of such overwhelming need. But the girl was insistent—she wanted to do what she could. The pastor wisely accepted the small and seemingly insignificant gift.

But the story doesn't end there.

When the church heard about this simple act, coats, scarves, hats, mittens and gloves began coming into the church. And other needed items as well—furniture, appliances, beds, etc., until when all was said and done, that small rural church had filled an entire semi for the reservation.

But that still wasn't the end of the story.

That little, struggling congregation set a goal for the next year of filling two semis. And they did!

> *Truly I tell you, just as you did it to one of the least of these who are members of my family, you did it to me.*
>
> *—Matthew 25:40*

I find hope in that one small act. If one little girl can inspire that kind of change, then think what all of us together can accomplish! We can make a difference. And the ripple effect can change the world.

God's abundance

It was Sunday morning at the Bento Neusse UMC in Maputo, Mozambique. The church is situated in an area of dusty, rutted roads and small, poor homes. The church itself is simply a cinder block building with a corrugated metal roof. You could see daylight through many places where the roof and walls meet. There were no windows, only holes cut through the cinder blocks. Pieces of corrugated metal were nailed into place to cover the windows when the church was not in use. It was very clear: This was a poor church, in a very poor area, with seemingly little or no means beyond simply surviving.

And yet, as worship began, people kept coming and coming and coming until well over 250 people were crowded into that dingy, unpainted and very warm temple of God. This particular Sunday was a special day, as a group of United Methodist bishops were the invited guests. Churches from around the area had gathered to worship together.

During worship they celebrated birthdays and four people came forward—three children and one older couple. Each person (even an 11-year-old boy) witnessed to their faith, telling how God had blessed their lives, and then each gave a special offering in response to God's blessing. As the older couple began to speak, two young men came down the aisle carrying a window frame and this 75-year-old woman began to preach. She said (and I paraphrase): "God has blessed us with 75 years of life. We all take care of our homes, but here we sit in God's temple and we have no windows! As our gift to the church on my birthday, I give this window and I challenge you to do the same!" The choir started singing and one by one, people got up, walked to the front, and placed a special offering in the basket for the building fund of their church. Knowing how little these people had, I was deeply moved.

But there was more. As the time came for the regular offering, people were asked to come forward to place their gifts on the altar. The first people called forward were the tithers. They stood at the altar, gave their gifts, prayed over the basket of gifts and sang as they returned to their seats.

Next to come forward were the various local churches that had come for this celebration. Church by church they brought forward their offerings, each church singing their particular song of praise.

And the last group to come forward were the dignitaries—us. We came to the altar singing the song we had been taught for this moment, and as we did so, the entire congregation got up from their seats and came forward once again to give another gift to the church—singing all the way down and back. It was inspiring. And humbling.

As I watched people come forward, I couldn't help but think of how little they had, and yet how freely they gave. Out of so little, they could still praise God for God's abundant blessings and generously give back to God out of that faith.

> *And He looked up and saw the rich putting their gifts into the treasury, and He saw also a certain poor widow putting in two mites. So He said, "Truly I say to you that this poor widow has put in more than all; for all these out of their abundance have put in offerings for God, [a] but she out of her poverty put in all the livelihood that she had.*
>
> *—Luke 21:1-4*

As I said before—it's the people that give me hope for the Church.

Ordinary people, faithful people

I have met—and continue to meet—people across this denomination whose faith is so strong that when they have felt an urging, or a passion, or a whisper from God, they have changed the direction of their lives and literally changed the course of lives around them.

From starting a tutoring program in a small, rural church; to a shut-in who daily writes notes of encouragement to people in the community; to the woman who sells everything she has so she can begin seminary; to high-paying executives who give it all up and accept an appointment in a poverty-stricken neighborhood; to the creative spirit that sees the possibility of a church in a bar or a diner;to the faithful soul who faces death with a spirit of faith and joy; … and the list goes on.

These are the people I meet every day—common, ordinary people—who know what it means to live out their faith. It is in them—and their living out their faith—that I continue to find hope. In Hebrews 11:1, we read, *"Now faith is the assurance of things hoped for; the conviction of things not seen."* What follows is a list of the faithful—Abel, Enoch, Noah, Abraham, Moses, Gideon, Barak, Jephthah, David, Samuel and the prophets—each faithful in his or her own way.

But the list of the faithful doesn't end there. It continues with each and every one of us—each doing our part to bring in the kingdom of God. My hope is found in these faithful people—living common, ordinary lives, but carrying forward the faith. From excuse-offering Moses; to reluctant Jonah; to the least of the sons, David; to persecutor of the disciples, Saul; to tax collectors and fishermen; to you; and to me. All of us, ordinary folk, and yet, through them the faith was strengthened and it grew. *"On this rock,"* Jesus said, *"I will build my church and the gates of hell will not prevail against it"* (Matthew 16:18).

Like the cellist of Sarajevo, these people offer a glimpse of hope—a glimpse of what the Church is about—and what the Church can be. They are my sparks of hope that keep my faith alive and rekindled when so many other circumstances would extinguish it. They remind me that hope, and wisdom, and discipleship, and grace, and peace can be found throughout the people of God. And I am grateful.

That is my hope.

Thanks be to God!

—Bishop Deborah Lieder Kiesey

Bishop Deborah Lieder Kiesey is the episcopal leader for the Michigan Area that includes the Detroit and West Michigan Annual Conferences. Previously she served as the bishop of the Dakotas Area and as a pastor and district superintendent in the Iowa Annual Conference. She is a graduate of Morningside College and Boston University School of Theology. She holds honorary degrees from Iowa Wesleyan College and Dakota Wesleyan University and currently serves on the board of trustees at Adrian College.

CHAPTER 10

Facing the Future Unafraid; the Voices of Young Leaders

THE WORD OF the angels to Joseph, Mary and the shepherds began with the command, *"Do not be afraid."* So we have heard the voices of selected bishops of the Church offering the same words of hope for this day and for the future of United Methodism. They speak from years of experience and in their role as ordained elders, pastors, teachers and episcopal leaders. From the secular culture of Northern Europe and the West Coast of the U.S. to the emerging Church in Africa; from the Sun Belt to the Rust Belt, they have offered their words of hope.

But now, what about a word from the leaders of the future, those who have responded to God's call and have dedicated themselves to the task in this day? What about the young clergy whose experience in the Church does not hark back to the salad days of the '50s, or the excitement of the '60s, but rather have come to their calling in the first decade of the 21st century when the Church seems to march to the constant drumbeat of decline and demise. Even so, they still come with hope and passion, to use an old-fashioned word—zeal! Where does it come from? Where do these young leaders find their ability to face the future without fear?

The following contributors represent this new generation of young leaders. They represent a variety of backgrounds, geographic regions and theological schools. Together they offer a vision for the future and the promise for the Church.

~

The Rev. Chris McAlilly, Mississippi

Chris goes right to the heart of it. He finds his hope in the creative power of God. Chris is a recent graduate of Candler School of Theology in Atlanta, GA, currently serving in his first appointment as the pastor of the Shannon and Brewer United Methodist Churches in the Mississippi Annual Conference. He is the chair of the Board of Discipleship.

Hope in the creative action of God

I am the son and grandson of United Methodist clergy, so I have seen the Church at its best and at its worst. I have seen the Church fully alive and I have seen the Church on the doorstep of becoming the "dead sect" that Wesley worried about late in his life. My hope in ministry is rooted in the ongoing creative action of God to give life. Dr. Luke Timothy Johnson, my professor of New Testament at Candler School of Theology, wrote in his exposition of the Creed that to affirm that God is the creator of heaven and earth is not simply a statement about the divine artistry and ingenuity evident at the very beginning, but a confession about the vibrancy of God's ongoing creative action. Nowhere is God's continuing capacity to create expressed more clearly than in the resurrection of Jesus from the dead. A new creation is born out of ashes and death. My hope is found in a God who has the capacity to say: *"Behold, I make all things new!"*

I see evidence of new life and resurrection around me all the time, especially among persons who allow their lives to become channels of the life-giving Spirit of God. I see it in my organic farming friends who have devoted themselves to the slow work of soil restoration on an old sunbaked soybean field that had been stripped of its nutrients by industrial chemicals and pesticides. I see it in my congregation as they respond to God's call to participate in the restorative work of the kingdom in a declining public school system. I sense the Spirit breathing new life into our denomination as a new generation of United Methodist scholars like Jason Vickers, Andrew Thompson, Elaine Heath and Kevin Watson attempt to recover a distinctive Wesleyan identity and witness. I have seen the living faith of John and Charles Wesley alive in The United Methodist Church through them.

So, what sustains me in ministry? Not the naïve belief that my actions will be enough to hold back death, tsunamis and declining numbers which have plagued The United Methodist Church since the 1960s. My hope resides with the God who promises to make all things new and who prompts us to remember the action and energy that animated the living faith of the saints.

~

The Rev. Romonica Malone-Wardley, Texas

Many of our young African-American pastors find themselves serving in congregations that face the current issues related to urban violence and the place of young African-American males in our society. Romonica shares words of hope that are grounded in the witness of her grandmother and the voices of the young men around her. She is currently serving the Blue Ridge United Methodist Church, Houston, TX. Her husband is also an ordained clergy and serves as campus pastor.

Growing up, we did not have much. There were no books in my house, other than the Bible. We did not take vacations or visit museums. In fact, my family worked hard at low-paying jobs just to make ends meet. Until I was in middle school, the majority of our clothes were hand-me-downs from my cousins.

I spent a lot of my time as a young child with my grandmother. I believed she was magical! Who else could go into a kitchen that would be described as bare and create what we thought was a feast? Some flour and eggs, vegetables that often came from a neighbor's garden, meat smothered or fried and always a song of praise on her lips. I remember waking up to my grandmother reading her Bible and kneeling beside the bed to pray at night. She went to church every Sunday, sometimes twice if there were special programs. She and her neighbors checked on each other and shared what little they had. My grandmother was a person of hope.

Hope is one of those words we generally use when things are not good: *I hope things get better; I hope the prognosis is good; I hope things change.* But in Romans chapter 5 it says:

> *We boast in our hope of sharing the glory of God. And not only that, but we also boast in our sufferings, knowing that suffering produces endurance, and endurance produces character and character produces hope and hope does not disappoint us, because God's love has been poured into our hearts through the Holy Spirit that has been given to us.*

Several weeks ago after Wednesday night Bible study, a group of youth walked across the street and stood in a large circle where people called out prayer concerns before we prayed together. An 11th grader raised his hand, as if he were in a classroom, and asked if he could share a prayer concern. He asked us to pray for one of his classmates who had been shot. We stopped and lifted his friend up in prayer. That Wednesday night, as he walked away from me all I could think about was the recent news reports, protests and concerns over the lives of our young African-American males. My love and hope for the Church is that we continue to be a safe place where this young man and the other children who walk across the street with no parents can come to encounter an Incarnate Savior and know they are beloved.

So, for me, the Church is not the place to run from in times of trouble and difficulty. Rather it is to the Church to which we should run. I see signs of resurrection in the Church's ability to stand with young African-Americans who are lost, suffering, broken-hearted, and experiencing injustice.

Recently, when I arrived at Blue Ridge as the new pastor, we scheduled a series of small group gatherings in members' homes. One of the questions I asked was, "What do you think breaks God's heart in our neighborhood?" That question led every group to a discussion about our youth and young people and particularly our African-American boys and men. After those meetings, the United Methodist men scheduled a meeting with the principal of a local elementary school to ask how our church can support them. They left that meeting and met with my husband, a campus minister, to offer support to college students. The United Methodist men understand that if we start at the elementary school level, we can positively influence youth before they get to the 11th grade. They also understand that college students still need support and encouragement. They are men of hope.

I grew up with a grandmother who believed she was blessed. Not because she had an abundance of material possessions, but because of her relationship with God and her community. She knew that no matter what was going on in her life, she was not alone. And while she *hoped* that one day things would get better, she also praised God in the midst of her circumstances and sought to be a blessing to others. Therefore, even as I look at these times of darkness, despair, apathy and hatred, times when it can be scary to hear about churches closing, the rising number of the "nones," (the number of Americans who do not identify with any religion) and decline in Church membership, I see signs of hope in the lives of young men and in the remembrance of my grandmother. For God has not given us a spirit of fear. He has given us the power of the Holy Spirit to spread his message to the ends of the earth. Not only are we not alone, but we have the power to tell broken people from all walks of life to pick up their mats and walk. That is good news! That is hope. And in that hope, we need not live in fear.

~

The Rev. Jiyeon Kim, Virginia

Jiyeon's story represents the joy and the challenges of cross-cultural appointment and our desire to be a fully inclusive Church. A native of South Korea, she brings the passion and the commitment of the Korean Church to her ministry, but she has also confronted the difficult barriers of language and cultural differences in the American Church. As a woman in pastoral ministry, she is also the exception in the Korean Church. Her strong sense of call has been the anchor for her in this journey.

Yes, it's me! Thank God!

I was born in a faithful Methodist family in South Korea and came to America in August 2009, at the age of 23, with a serious aspiration to be "an influential female leader of the world." However, it was not easy to live as a young person leaving the beloved parental roof and as a foreigner in an unfamiliar environment. When I graduated from Wesley Theological Seminary and began my ministry in the summer of 2012, I realized ministry is much harder than study.

I definitely feel called to be set apart by God to do the work of God. I truly believe God has led me to this point and that in order to fulfill what He is calling me to do and to respond to the call, it can be only achieved by my service in ministry. I served Chesterbrook United Methodist Church in McLean, VA, as a seminarian pastor for two years while I was in the seminary. For the next two years, as a licensed local pastor, I served Charlotte United Methodist Charge in Charlotte County, VA. As of June 25, 2014, I have been appointed to Warrenton United Methodist Church in Warrenton, VA as an associate pastor. Even though I have been eager to be in ministry for a long time, I have faced many difficulties and challenges in ministry, which are mostly caused by my different background, language barrier and insufficient cultural understanding of the American Methodist Church. There were numerous moments that something basic I had done without any problem became something difficult. I had to struggle against low self-esteem and self-confidence in my dream and gifts.

Thankfully, now I can say that through those experiences I learned humility as a servant and absolute dependence on God. Strange eyes from others, because of my noticeable difference, still often hurt me and freeze my passion of ministry. However, when I am again convinced of God's purpose and will in my life and ministry, all doubts in my heart disappear. I find hope in ministry by serving the Church of God and the people of God. I know difference is not a weakness, but a special strength. My ministry has shown the obvious way that God wants me to go, and I am able to do, obey and follow the calling. As a person in a cross-cultural ministerial setting, I constantly ask God's purpose and will, asking *why* God chooses and uses me, and *what* God wants to do by using my difference and gifts. God and the people of God keep me moving toward ministry and staying in ministry where my gifts are needed even if they are not perfect.

Today, in this society, we share more diverse experiences created by racial, cultural, socioeconomic, religious and generational differences. The diversity has provoked serious conflicts and isolated persons/groups in society, even in our faith communities. It becomes a real issue in the Church. I remember the inclusiveness and openness of Paul's missionary journeys and the moments Jesus reached out his hands toward the weak and the different. They knew difference is not wrong. It is not because of who I am, but because who God is, that I have welcomed, invited and embraced in this strange land. Of course, it does not mean everyone gladly welcomes me and opens their hearts and minds to me at first. Even though it took a long time to regard my difference as a special gift, I learned that difference is neither a wrong nor a fault, but it makes God's world more colorful and powerful. I also learned God's viewpoint of the world, which is not limited to a specific time and space, culture or nation, but expands to the whole world and future. As close-minded hearts are broken and embrace more people just as they are, I pray for the time when everyone sees each other's hearts. Not visible appearance and background, but inner beauty and stories.

In The United Methodist Church we believe we are the Church of "open hearts, open minds, open doors." I truly believe that there is no outsider and no stranger in Jesus Christ. This is my hope for the Church. I pray for the oneness of the Church and the wholeness of the world. The Church needs to strive for unity and communion with a strong belief in God's work through the Holy Spirit. I envision a Church that embraces all the diversity of the society and shows the universal grace of God for everyone through its mission and ministry. I believe in the power of the Holy Spirit working through me and my special identity. For I am young—I bring youthfulness. For I am a stranger—I bring refreshing insights and diversity. Yes, I am different. It's me! Thank God who made me in this way and uses me just as I am!

~

The Rev. Jared Kindall, Indiana

Jared grew up in Indiana and Michigan and graduated from Indiana Wesleyan College. He received his Master of Divinity from Duke Divinity School and is currently serving his first appointment at Otterbein United Methodist Church in Lebanon,

IN. Jared looks to our Wesleyan roots and the tradition of baptism as the foundation for his ministry and his hope for the future of the Church.

Hope rooted in our Methodist traditions

How do I respond to the mood of the Church in these times of turmoil and division? What moves me toward ministry in these days? Where do I see hope? These are difficult questions because I am growing increasingly frustrated with the "doom and gloom" narrative that bombards me from every denominational gathering, conference communication and my Twitter feed.

Nobody wants to board a sinking ship. So, when I hear every conference reporting how many people we've lost and when I notice how few 20-somethings are present in the clergy session, I admittedly wonder why I am doing ministry within our denomination. My response is rooted in my hope in Christ, the relationships formed in local churches that have shaped my love for Christ and because I whole-heartedly believe our distinctive Wesleyan theological heritage offers a "meatier" alternative for those who have left the Church.

Hope expressed in our baptism and resurrection

My ethics professor at Duke Divinity School used to remind our class: "Dear students, you're already dead." It was an unsettling remark that invited us to live into our baptisms. And so, whenever people lament our "dying" denomination, I am reminded of my baptism. Perhaps, more specifically, I am reminded of Easter. I actually believe God came to the world in Jesus, that Jesus *"was crucified, dead, and buried"* and on *"the third day he rose from the dead."* If we United Methodists still espouse such an understanding, we would spend less time and resources lamenting our dying and more on identifying the continual reflections of Easter's resurrection that are unfolding around us. And so, when conversations turn the route of doom and gloom, I try to remind people that we are an Easter people. There is always hope for us who have died with Christ to also be raised to new life with Him. There is always hope because of Jesus. Nothing and no one is beyond the scope of God's redemption and resurrection … not even our denomination. And so, in response to those who proclaim our impending doom, I am reminded that I am already dead. I am reminded of my baptism. And I am reminded of the profound hope I have in the God revealed in Jesus Christ.

Hope rooted in our Wesleyan story

Finally, my hope is shaped by my belief that our distinct Wesleyan theological emphasis offers a richer alternative to the American Church, particularly its young people who have walked away. I grew up in an evangelical environment and I am grateful for that upbringing and the way it has rooted me in Christ, but I have also experienced some of the "unsavory" aspects of it as well. I have had many friends who walked away because their faith was seemingly incapable of responding to their increasingly complex worlds. Too often, the response to life's gray areas was a simplistic black or white answer. I believe our beliefs as United Methodists allow for life's difficult questions and reinforce our belief in loving God with our hearts, souls, our strength and our minds. We can, therefore, wrestle with life's gray areas in ways that are faithful to the Gospel message while also offering meatier reasons for why things exist as they do. Our emphasis on the balance between personal piety and social responsibility speaks directly to a culture that longs to punch a "ticket to heaven" and neglect caring for this world. Our Wesleyan tradition implores us to be concerned with justice ministries, caring for creation and engaging the realities of our present time with the hope of Christ's resurrection.

So when I hear the longings of younger families, I take great joy in sharing the beauty of our faith tradition. I love helping others see God's unfolding Easter kingdom and I have great hope that God will continue to raise up United Methodists to "reform the nation, particularly the Church and spread scriptural holiness throughout the land."

~

The Rev. Megan Crumm Walther, Michigan

An ordained elder in the Detroit Conference of The United Methodist Church, Megan is the granddaughter of the late Rev. Donald Crumm, who at the time of her ordination as one of the youngest elders in the Conference, held the "Conference cane" as the oldest living elder in the Detroit Conference. Megan and her husband, the Rev. Joel Walther, graduated from Wesley Theological Seminary in Washington, D.C. She was appointed to a rural parish and he was appointed to two in Southern Michigan. Megan shares a word about another part of our Methodist story, the power of community. In Wesley's day they were known as Class Meetings, Bands and Societies. Today, that sense of community is expressed in small groups, Sunday school classes and caring ministries. In this experience Megan discovered once again the power of community to offer comfort and to provide hope.

A phone call in the night

Late one Saturday night, I got a phone call. A longtime church member had died unexpectedly. The family asked me to come to the house and wait with them until the funeral director arrived to pick up the body. When I arrived, the house was already full of people from the congregation. Every few minutes the door would open and another church member would arrive. When we stood together to pray, the circle filled the living room.

People are the Body of Christ, and the Spirit moves in community. More than 200 years ago, small bands of men and women spread the Methodist community across the emerging United States. Yes, our denomination rests on the Wesleys' early inspiration and the courage of Francis Asbury and the early circuit riders, but our strength has always been faithful people in small communities.

Late on a Saturday night in my small town, the people called United Methodists had dropped everything to be with this family. These relationships—and this love—was formed through our church. In the midst of tragedy, there was something beautiful: because of the church, this family did not have to grieve alone. I have hope for the Church because of moments like these.

~

The Rev. Scott Chrostek, Kansas

"Resurrection Downtown" is one of the exciting signs of new life in the Church today. It was founded as a satellite of Kansas City's United Methodist Church of the Resurrection pastored by the well-known Dr. Adam Hamilton. When Hamilton was looking for a young pastor to plant a new congregation in the heart of the city, he invited Scott to take on the task. Scott, a native of Michigan, and his wife the Rev. Wendy Chrostek, originally from Louisiana, met at Duke Divinity School. At UMC of the Resurrection, Wendy assumed responsibility for pastoral care and Scott planted "RezDowntown." He tells the story of his calling in his first published book, Pursuit: Living Fully in Search of God's Presence. Scott anchors his faith and hope for the Church in the

promises of God from Scripture and he invites us to do the same with the simple question, "Do you believe?"

Do you believe this?

I believe that by the grace of God we have the power to do extraordinary things. Each of us is created and called to open ourselves to the power of Christ so that we can change the world in extraordinary ways. We can become like Christ and reflect the image of God in a way that invites others to do the same until, eventually, this world will be transformed, redeemed and reconciled back to God.

Doing greater things

In John 14, Jesus predicts his own gruesome death. With the shock of this news settling in, the disciples were blinded by profound grief. And yet, in this dark and despairing moment, he urges his disciples to take action and go to work. He also makes this amazing promise: *"The one who believes in me will also do the works that I do and, in fact, will do greater works than these"* (John 14:12). In the midst of that night of darkness, Jesus tells his disciples that by the power of the Holy Spirit they will eventually do the same things he will do. In fact, Jesus says, *"They will do even greater works than these."* Is that what you'd expect to hear in that moment? When the chips are down, do expect to hear words of strength and power? How would you respond? I guess the better question is would you believe this?

In Ephesians 3, the apostle Paul says something similar. From prison he uses words that mirror Christ's remarks in the Gospel of John when he says:

I pray that, according to the riches of his glory, Christ may grant that you may be strengthened in your inner being with power through his Spirit, and that Christ may dwell in your hearts through faith, as you are being rooted and grounded in love. I pray that you may have the power to comprehend, with all the saints, what is the breadth and length and height and depth, and to know the love of Christ that surpasses knowledge, so that you may be filled with all the fullness of God.

—*Ephesians 3:16-19*

Then, without skipping a beat, Paul continues by praying, *"Now to him who by the power at work within us is able to accomplish abundantly far more than all we can ask or imagine"* (Ephesians 3:20).

He promises that when we are filled with the fullness of God, we are able to accomplish abundantly far more than all we can ask or imagine, to do "greater things." Do you believe this?

Hope for the Church today

The word Christ offers his disciples facing the cross and the word Paul shares with a community under fire are the words I hang onto when thinking about the call Christ has placed on the lives of all his disciples. Jesus and Paul said that by the power of Christ at work in us, we can do exceedingly abundant, great things even when the day seems darkest. I believe this applies to the Church at this time of darkness, doubt and uncertainty. Now is the time to go to work. Now is the time to believe in the power of God. Now is the time to live fully into the future-loving God with everything we have and doing the same for our neighbors to the extent that God might be glorified and the earth and everything in it restored. Jesus says we will do *"greater works."* Paul promises we can do *"exceedingly abundant above all we can ask or think."*

Do you believe this? Sometimes, I wonder what would happen if a whole community of people believed this.

~

Will and Ella Faircloth, Costa Rica

Will and Ella bring a unique perspective to the conversation with young leaders about the future of the Church. Natives of the Deep South, they grew up with little background in the global mission. After graduating from Duke Divinity School, they accepted the invitation of the bishop of the Methodist Church of Costa Rica to teach in the seminary. They have invested themselves in the work of both the seminary and the building of the Methodist Children's Home of Costa Rica. Will's hope for the future of the Church lies in his vision of shared global ministry under the guidance of the Holy Spirit.

My calling in global missions

I must confess that we are missionaries with no deep roots in the field. Rather, quite the opposite. Raised as a Methodist in wonderfully typical UMC congregations in Alabama and Mississippi, I cannot remember a single time that a missionary visited nor a single Sunday school class devoted to mission work around the globe. My own family members were faithful members of the Church and often participated in nearby service projects. I went on mission trips with my UMYF group. These experiences helped give me awareness of others' needs and of the Christian duty to serve, but none of this was framed in a broader discussion of the global Church. In retrospect, it does seem like a notable absence for a people who claim "the world is our parish." Where was the institutional Church making its global mission voice heard, creating awareness and raising support for Methodist work around the world?

Relevant, too, is the timing of my upbringing in the Church. In the mid-'90s in southern Mississippi, the farthest-flung idea for a youth trip was to spend a week working in an African-American community in north Mississippi or perhaps rural Appalachia. The idea of a youth foreign mission trip, now so common, was not on our radar. Yet this period, the mid-'90s, was right at the tipping point of the trend toward foreign mission trips as the major youth activity in many local churches. Now, it is commonplace for local Methodist youth groups to find their own project to support through a work trip and mission team experience. This isn't just a phenomenon for the youth groups, however, as whole congregations have been reaching out in their desire to be directly involved in foreign missions.

This story of my own ignorance of foreign missions laid the groundwork for my eventual call to work in international mission service. After graduating from Duke Divinity School, my wife and I were invited by the bishop of the Evangelical Methodist Church of Costa Rica to come and work within their country. This calling led us outside the traditional structure of United Methodist Board of Global Ministries into a somewhat uncertain, yet challenging, opportunity. We have now invested our lives in this country and have adopted two Costa Rican daughters. We feel we are truly a part of the Methodist Church of Costa Rica and intend to live out our calling in this place.

Hope for the future of the global Church

My hope for the future of the global Methodist movement in world missions is a hope grounded in the Holy Spirit. The Spirit that calls some people to invest their lives serving abroad is the same the Spirit that tells an insurance salesman or a schoolteacher to give up their summer vacation and go dig a well in the Guatemalan highlands. This is the same

Spirit that took a group of charismatic disciples and turned them into an ordered church. It's the same Spirit that had the congregation at Antioch send out Paul and Barnabas as missionaries to the Gentiles and told Paul to take up a collection among the Gentiles for the starving saints in Jerusalem. Today, this same Spirit works within systems without being constrained by them; in the partnership between local churches, Annual Conferences and autonomous regional Methodist denominations; and in the lives of individuals who respond to the call. I see hope for global missions both within and without the traditional structures as this same Spirit moves today.

~

The Rev. Tori Butler, campus chaplain at Wiley College, Texas

Tori was raised by her mother in Baltimore who told her: "If you are bored, go read a book. It can take you wherever you want to go." She became the first of her peer group from her neighborhood to get a college degree when she graduated from McDaniel College with a degree in international relations. During a semester abroad in Argentina, she sensed a call to ministry. After graduating from Duke Divinity School, she served two cross-racial appointments before becoming the chaplain at Wiley College in Marshall, TX, a historically black college related to The United Methodist Church. Tori brings her passion to be a "prophet, preacher, activist, evangelist, counselor, shouter and dancer" to her work in campus ministry. If Methodism is to have a claim on the next generation, it will be in part because of persons like Tori who commit their lives to crossing the racial barriers of our society and reaching college students through campus ministry. She shares a word of promise and hope for the future.

The best is yet to come

One day, while watching public access television, I happened to catch an address by Senator Cory Booker who, at the time, was the mayor of Newark, NJ. Senator Booker talked about how, after graduating from Yale, he felt a call to go and live in the Cabrini Housing Projects in Newark. These projects had a horrible reputation of being dilapidated and crime-ridden. Nevertheless, Cory answered the call to go and be a part of the community.

He contacted the local community organizer who gave him a tour of the neighborhood. While giving the tour, the woman asked him, "What do you see?" He began to give her a description of the drug dealers on the corner, the boarded up houses and the prostitutes. He told her everything that was wrong with the community. The woman turned and looked at him. Then she said, "You cannot help me."

Cory was quick to respond saying, "What do you mean I cannot help you? I am young. I am energetic. I am from Yale."

She told him, "If all you can see is the negative and not the possibilities, than you can't help me."

I have to admit that I have been like Cory and many other young people looking at our denomination, and all I could see was the negative. I have a been a part of The United Methodist Church since I was 7 years old when my neighbor Miss Trudy walked me to church on Sunday morning—many times without my mother. My experience within the Church has not always been positive.

I have witnessed/been a part of a dying congregation with an old building that was falling apart. It had no heat in the winter and no cool air in the summer. I have sat in church services where the congregation expected young people to conform to a 19th century model of worship, even though they were a part of the technology age of the 21st century. I have sat in seminary classes geared to prepare young United Methodists leaders and noticed out of classes of 75 students, I was the only African-American face in the room. I have been a part of a church where the outreach was limited to a soup kitchen on Tuesdays even though we were across the street from a high school and within walking distance of two elementary schools. I have to confess I wrestled with being a part of a denomination that I did not always see being the local church in mission; or providing opportunities for passionate worship; or plainly celebrating the gift of diversity. When I heard the words of the communion liturgy that "Christ invites all to the table," I began to wonder: Does the all include me? Does this all include someone who believes in the power of the Holy Spirit? Does this all include someone who was not born to privilege? Does this all include someone who did not have the traditional United Methodist pedigree?

But, in the midst of my questioning, I heard the voice of God tell me that I was called to this Church. I was called to be a part of the something new that God wanted to do within our denomination.

However, I could not be a part of the something new if I did not know who we were and why we came to be. Through my Methodism courses in seminary, I began to understand that John Wesley and a group of his friends were tired of the Church not being the Church. So they went into the fields and into the jail cells and preached that God's grace was available to all through faith in Jesus Christ. As I began to study John Wesley, I fell in love with the United Methodist theology of grace. I believed that the grace of God went before me and saved me and continued to sanctify me each and every day. I believed that our theology was something that was timeless. And if I could live into whom we said that we are, then I believed that maybe this denomination was not done after all.

When the prophet Ezekiel received his vision of the valley of the very dead and dry bones, the Lord asked him, *"Can these bones live?"*

His response was, *"Only you know God."* God told Ezekiel to prophesy to the bones. And it was in the prophesying that what was once dead came back to life. I believe that we are a denomination in which resurrection is still a part of our very being. I believe that our denomination has a place for all at the table. However, I do believe that there is a need for revival. I do believe we have to work harder for the marginalized and the disenfranchised of the world to feel as if they have a place at the table.

As a young African-American elder in the United Methodist Church, I have hope in the unseen. I have hope in a God who is able to do exceedingly and abundantly beyond what any of us can think or imagine. I know that God is not through with our denomination yet. I truly believe the best is yet to come and I am so glad to be a part of it.

Conclusion

THE ANGELIC MESSENGERS visited faithful shepherds doing the hard and sometimes unappreciated work of keeping watch over their flock in the darkness of night. They came with the greeting, *"Fear not. Behold, we bring you glad tidings of great joy which shall be to all people."* So this group of episcopal messengers have offered their word of "glad tidings" to faithful lay and clergy servants, many of whom feel like they are keeping watch in the darkness of night, serving dwindling flocks of aging saints, confronting unspeakable tragedy in the world with seemingly little effect, reading the sobering statistics and listening to the unsettling voices calling for schism. As the chosen episcopal leaders of the Church, they have shared where they see glimmers of light, evidence of resurrection and hope for the Church. We did not ask for their commentary on the issues that divide us or the fears that inhibit us, we asked for images that might inspire us and examples that might engage us in our search for a hopeful future.

Then we asked a group of young clergy why they would enter ministry in a time such as this. Where do they find inspiration for their calling and passion for their ministry? Where do they hear the still, small voice saying, *"Do not be afraid"*? These young men and women will be leading the Church through the decades ahead and will do so with courage and zeal. They represent our best hope, hope that comes from someplace much deeper than reading the statistical tea leaves, hope that comes from their calling to serve.

Is it fair to ask, "Are we just whistling through the grave-yard, trying to buck up our spirits in hopes of keeping the flock together and holding off the night?" Perhaps. No one is denying the realities of our times. The 40-plus-year decline of membership in the United States has been the backdrop of our life together since the merger in 1968. Our internal turmoil over social issues, like homosexuality, has filled our inboxes with commentary and divided congregations as well as Conferences. The last General Conference was, in the view of many, an all-time low in our life together as the United Methodist Connection. The predictions for 2016 General Conference offer little hope of a better example of "Holy Con-ferencing." The bishops and young clergy who have shared in this project are well aware of the state of the Church. In spite of that, or perhaps because of that, our contributors were eager and willing to speak words of glad tidings, good news and, perhaps, even great joy. And is that not the story of the Church throughout 2,000 years of history—miracles of heal-ing in the most hopeless of situations, the hungry being fed from just five loaves and three small fishes, Good Friday giv-ing way to Easter morning, even the blood of the martyrs becoming the seed of the Church? The Church is always look-ing for light in the darkness and resurrection, even in the places of death.

In 1988, the United Methodist Church adopted a new hym-nal. For hymnody, it has served us well. However, there was one subtle and significant loss. In the previous hymnal, the liturgy for confirmation and the reception of new members began with these powerful words:

Dearly beloved, the Church is of God, and will be preserved to the end of time for the conduct of worship and the due administration of Word and Sacraments, the maintenance of Christian fellowship and discipline, the edification of believers and the conversation of the world. All persons of every age and station stand in the need of the means of grace which the church alone supplies (UM Hymnal 1964, #829).

There it is. Beneath our personal aspirations and hopes, deeper than our deepest divisions and doubts our conviction is that "The Church is of God, and will be preserved till the end of time." Our hope, our ultimate assurance and the antidote for fear comes from a bedrock understanding of the church as the Body of Christ whose future rests not only on our words and actions, but on the very Word of God.

The question for us in our times is not whether "the Church" will be preserved till the end of time, but whether Methodism will be preserved as a vital and living part of the ongoing movement of God's people through time and history. Certainly, John Wesley and Frances Asbury believed that it would. Methodism spread throughout England, the United States of America and around the world on the confidence and courage of circuit riders, preachers, missionaries and teachers. These were men and women who were willing to face the challenges of their times with hope and determination.

In 1971, Dr. Albert Outler delivered the Denman Lectures at the Congress on Evangelism in New Orleans. He raised the same question about the future of Methodism and the hope for what he called the "Third Great Awakening." He described his day, and perhaps ours, as a time of "suspended animation," a time of the "slow decline of the kind of post-Constantinian Christianity which is already passé" (*Evangelism in the Wesleyan Spirit*, Tidings press, 1971, page 82). However, he concluded with a stirring statement of hope for the future based on the life and work of ordinary men and women seeking to be faithful witnesses in their sphere of influence:

> *Give us a church whose members believe and understand the Gospel of God's healing love in Christ to hurting men and women. Give us a church that speaks and acts in consonance with its faith—not only to reconcile the world but to turn it upside down! Give us a church of spirit-filled people in whose fellowship life speaks to life, love to love, and faith and trust respond to God's grace. And we shall have a church whose witness in the world will not fail and whose service to the world will transform it. What can you do, what can the Methodist people do to give us such a church?*
>
> —*Evangelism in the Wesleyan Spirit,* **Tidings Press, 1971, page 56**

If Methodism is to endure, it will be because of faithful servants and shepherds who look for the angelic messengers and listen for the words "*Do not be afraid.*" It will be because of courageous bishops and young clergy who are willing to share the glad tidings of great joy. It will be because of committed laypeople in every congregation who look for the signs of resurrection and serve in ways that effectively make disciples of Jesus Christ for the transformation of the world. We pray for that kind of Church.

CPSIA information can be obtained at www.ICGtesting.com
Printed in the USA
BVOW04s1153050515

398982BV00002B/6/P

9 781939 880963